# Ethnohistory

Volume 66, Number 4
October 2019

Special Issue: Mesoamerican Experiences of Illness and Healing
*Edited by Rebecca Dufendach*

## Articles

"As if His Heart Died": A Reinterpretation of Moteuczoma's
Cowardice in the Conquest History of the Florentine
Codex   *Rebecca Dufendach*   623

Tepahtihquetl pan ce pilaltepetzin / A Village Healer
*Sabina Cruz de la Cruz*
*Translated by Rebecca Dufendach*   647

Ossified and Materialized Selves in Three Manuscripts of Colonial
Guatemala: Connections with the Sacred Instrumentality
of Bone   *Servando Z. Hinojosa*   667

The Serpent Within: Birth Rituals and Midwifery Practices
in Pre-Hispanic and Colonial Mesoamerican Cultures
*Gabrielle Vail*   689

Perinatal Rites in the *Ritual of the Bacabs*, a Colonial
Maya Manuscript   *Timothy W. Knowlton*
*and Edber Dzidz Yam*   721

## Book Reviews

Laurent Corbeil: The Motions Beneath: Indigenous Migrants
of the Urban Frontier of New Spain   *Susan M. Deeds*   745

Jonathan Truitt: Sustaining the Divine in Mexico Tenochtitlan: Nahuas and Catholicism, 1523–1700   *William F. Connell*   748

Fernando Santos-Granero: Slavery and Utopia: The Wars and Dreams of an Amazonian World Transformer, and Stephen L. Nugent: The Rise and Fall of the Amazon Rubber Industry: An Historical Anthropology   *Robert Wasserstrom*   750

Yuko Miki: Frontiers of Citizenship: A Black and Indigenous History of Postcolonial Brazil   *James P. Woodard*   753

Lisa Brooks: Our Beloved Kin: A New History of King Philip's War   *Jon Parmenter*   755

James K. Barnett, ed.: Captain Cook's Final Voyage: The Untold Story from the Journals of James Burney and Henry Roberts   *David Igler*   757

Rob Harper: Unsettling the West: Violence and State Building in the Ohio Valley   *Rebecca Kugel*   759

Joshua S. Haynes: Patrolling the Border: Theft and Violence on the Creek-Georgia Frontier, 1770–1796   *Steven J. Peach*   761

Michelle A. Lelièvre: Unsettling Mobility: Mediating Mi'kmaw Sovereignty in Post-contact Nova Scotia   *Catherine M. Cameron*   763

Ann McGrath: Illicit Love: Interracial Sex and Marriage in the United States and Australia   *Brandon Layton*   765

Richard Ravalli: Sea Otters: A History   *John Ryan Fischer*   767

Harvey Markowitz: Converting the Rosebud: Catholic Mission and the Lakotas, 1886–1916   *David C. Posthumus*   769

# "As if His Heart Died": A Reinterpretation of Moteuczoma's Cowardice in the Conquest History of the Florentine Codex

Rebecca Dufendach, *Getty Research Institute*

**Abstract.** The first encounters between Nahuas and Spaniards from 1519 to 1521 resulted in widespread deaths in the indigenous communities of central Mexico. Although the first recorded disease epidemic is often acknowledged as a factor in the loss of rule to the invaders, Moteuczoma receives much of the blame. Historians contend that Moteuczoma's cowardice facilitated the defeat of his people. Instead, this article argues that descriptions of the pain and fright that afflicted Moteuczoma and his people in Book XII of the Florentine Codex are references to long-standing cultural concepts of illness. This article uses colonial and modern ethnographic sources to illuminate enduring Mesoamerican concepts of health and sickness. The chaos and loss of life connected to the first epidemic in 1520 contributed significantly to the fall of Tenochtitlan. This article reveals how Nahuas remembered and understood the startling arrival of the Spaniards and the first terrifying disease epidemic during the invasion.

**Keywords.** Mexico, Nahuas, Nahuatl, Moteuczoma, epidemic, disease, conquest, Florentine Codex

## Introduction

In the search to understand the mythic history of how a handful of Spaniards conquered the Aztec empire, as so often the conquest of Mexico (1519–21) is portrayed, we focus on the actions of the "great men," or leaders. The *huei tlatoani* (great speaker) Moteuczoma Xocoyotzin (the Aztec ruler also known as Montezuma or Moctezuma) bears the brunt of the blame for the fall of the Mexica people. This article reexamines

*Ethnohistory* 66:4 (October 2019)  DOI 10.1215/00141801-7683240

depictions of Moteuczoma and the Mexica people in Book XII of the Florentine Codex through the lens of indigenous cultural concepts of illness. When viewed through Nahua concepts of illness, descriptions of fright should be reinterpreted as indications of failing health. This reinterpretation is crucial in framing how epidemic disease debilitated the Mexica's defensive abilities and leadership during the invasion of Tenochtitlan.

In order to place Moteuczoma's afflictions in the proper context, this article consults two sixteenth-century herbal manuscripts and modern ethnographic studies on the nature of health in indigenous communities. In both colonial and modern sources, Nahuas draw little distinction between emotional and physical ailments (see Cruz de la Cruz, this issue). Although centuries separate these two sets of sources, there are some fascinating similarities. Nahuatl speakers in the colonial period and in modern times adapted to outside influences and practices, but they also continued to rely on their own healers and methods of healing. Some of the best evidence for a continued reliance on traditional cures comes from the contemporary ethnographic record, where practices recorded in the early colonial period can be seen in contemporary indigenous communities (Huber and Sandstrom 2001). While acknowledging that Nahuas living and healing today may have adjusted or even changed their methods, their interpretations of fright illness are instructive when read alongside evidence from colonial times.[1] Only by situating Moteuczoma's afflictions in the cultural concepts of the colonial period, some of which have endured to the present day, can we understand the ruler's state of mind and body in the conquest history written by the indigenous authors of Book XII.

In their efforts to understand the conquest, scholars have portrayed a weak Mexica leader who could not bring himself to act. The infamous writings of William Prescott (1891: 223) that dominated the historical narrative of the conquest for many years referred to Moteuczoma as the leader of a "pusillanimous policy" that led to the downfall of the Nahua people. Prescott described the leader as "prey to the most dismal apprehensions" who "in a paroxysm of despair, shut himself up in his palace, refused food" (257). Prescott characterized Moteuczoma as a quaking and indecisive leader.

Similarly, James Lockhart (1993: 17) argued that portrayals of Moteuczoma's weakness were intended to make the tlatoani a scapegoat for the defeat of his people. Susan D. Gillespie (2008: 31) explained that "Moteuczoma was reduced to if not terror, at least profound anxiety." The figure of Moteuczoma was reduced to a weak state of emotional fragility. Gillespie detailed that Moteuczoma's frightful or cowardly actions represented methods used by indigenous authors to chronicle their resistance and accommodation to colonial rule. In his recent book on the history of the conquest, Mathew Restall (2018: 47) addresses the legends surrounding the figure of Moteuczoma. He acknowledges that one can easily imagine why Spanish accounts of the events portray the leader in a bad light but "it may be surprising, and is therefore more interesting, to discover that in the sixteenth century there developed among Nahua accounts a version of Montezuma the Coward." In his examination of the Nahuatl language record, Kevin Terraciano (2014: 225) finds that the negative portrayals of the leader can be attributed to the rivalry between the group to which Moteuczoma belonged, the Tenocha, and the Tlatelolcans, the group to which many of the codex authors and elders belonged. While discussing modern celebrations and the iconography of Mexican identity, Jaime Cuadriello (2009: 119) explains that "the 'coward' Moctezuma was altogether absent from the decorative scheme." Such interpretations equate fright with cowardice—a term with overwhelmingly negative connotations—and assume that it meant the same thing to Nahuas writing in the sixteenth century as it does to historians writing today. There is a great deal of material in the Nahuatl-language historical record that leads us to conclude that Moteuczoma was an ineffectual leader debilitated by fright.

Many of the scholars who highlight Moteuczoma's cowardice rely on the sixteenth-century text known as the Florentine Codex. Lockhart (1993: 17–18), in his introduction to his translation of Book XII, noted that the portrayal of Moteuczoma as "fawning and fearful" was a classic maneuver from a vanquished people searching for explanations. This article is not interested in whether the Mexica leader was or was not to blame for cowardice. More relevant are the oral traditions of Nahua elders and scholars that are recorded in the Florentine Codex, which, instead of solely illustrating cowardice, could indicate their memories of the leader as one who was suffering from poor health.

Collective Mexica memories of the Spaniards' arrival must have been influenced by the memories of the epidemics. Before contact in 1519, the estimated population of central Mexico was between 15 and 30 million people; it plummeted to 2 million people by 1600 (Cook and Simpson 1948: 43–55; Cook and Borah 1957; Gibson 1964: 593). Although scholars have acknowledged how warfare, colonial abuses, droughts, and famines contributed to this decline, epidemic diseases were the principal cause of death (Stahle et al. 2000; Acuna-Soto et al. 2002). Epidemic diseases were a defining characteristic of the colonial period, and as Amara Solari points out, Spanish colonists often conflated them with idolatry (2016: 507–8). Nahuas who survived the epidemics also explained poor health according to their own concepts of illness, which included heart pain and fright.

## Moteuczoma's Fright and Heart Failure in the Florentine Codex

Nahuas wrote their history of the conquest in Book XII of the Florentine Codex under the supervision of the Franciscan friar Bernardino de Sahagún. The codex consists of twelve books on a variety of topics, from Nahua cosmological beliefs and society to natural history and a history of the Spanish-led invasion of Tenochtitlan. Today the history found in Book XII is known as one of the most extensive indigenous accounts of the Spanish-led war on Mexico-Tenochtitlan (Terraciano 2010: 51). The text for the books resulted from a collaboration between Nahua elders and Nahua scholars trained to read and write in Nahuatl, Spanish, and Latin in the first European-style college in the Americas (Sahagún [1575–79] 1979: vol. 1, bk. XII, unmarked folio, note to the reader). The Nahua scholars Antonio Valeriano, Alonso Vegerano, Pedro de San Buenaventura, and Martín Jacobita sat with ten or twelve elders from Tlatelolco, a neighboring *altepetl* (ethnic city-state), to Tenochtitlan to understand their version of the invasion (Sahagún [1575–79] 1979: vol. 1, bk. II, fol. 1v). Sahagún explained that some of these men were alive during the war. Another set of Nahua scholars served as scribes for the project: Diego de Grado, Bonifacio Maximiliano, and Mateo Severino. The Nahua scholars, some elders, and Sahagún worked periodically from 1547 until 1577 to complete the texts that form the manuscript today known as the Florentine Codex.[2]

In Book XII, the Nahua elders and scholars depicted the suffering of Moteuczoma in a uniquely indigenous manner. The text explains that he sent a group of messengers to learn more about the Castilians, who arrived in boats at the coast. The Nahuatl text refers specifically to the health of Moteuczoma when the messengers returned and entered Tenochtitlan at night. The leader is said to have declared *vel patzmique in noiollo*, "my heart is squeezed to death" (Sahagún [1575–79] 1979: vol. 3, bk. XII, fol. 10v). The Nahua authors explained that Moteuczoma's heart suffered greatly. In addition to a crushed heart, Moteuczoma felt as though his heart had been doused with chili water, *chilatequilo* (vol. 3, bk. XII, fol. 10v). The text explained that his heart was burned and tormented. The torment only increased as the messengers relayed their findings on the threatening visitors.

The leader of Tenochtitlan received the contaminated messengers with appropriate caution. Moteuczoma ordered that two captives be slain and that their blood should be sprinkled using a small brush or broom on the messengers to cleanse them. The Nahua authors wrote in an uncharacteristic aside to the reader: "(The reason they did it was that they had gone to very dangerous places and had seen, gazed on the countenances of, and spoken to the gods)" (Sahagún [1575–79] 1979: vol. 3, bk. XII, fol. 10v).[3] This rare use of parentheses suggests that the explanation was needed to understand the serious nature of the messengers. The Nahuatl text uses the word *ohuican*, a word with several definitions according to the sixteenth-century *Vocabulario* written by an expert in Nahuatl, friar Alonso de Molina. Molina ([1571] 1977: 78 [second numeration]) defined it as "a dangerous place" or "a dark and scary place" (cf. Karttunen 1992: 177). The messengers experienced terrifying events and they were capable of spreading their contagion to others without proper cleansing. The Nahua authors took pains to explain why such protection was necessary for their leader. Moteuczoma was initially protected from the dangerous effects of the Spaniards.

The messengers, after the ceremony, related news that aggravated Moteuczoma's condition. The threatening news of the Spaniards and their powerful weapons caused him to faint, or, employing the Nahuatl verb *quiiolmicti*, "it made his heart die" (Sahagún [1575–79] 1979: vol. 3, bk. XII, fol. 11v). The authors of Book XII repeated their interpretations of Moteuczoma's reaction in the concluding paragraph. When he heard the news, he "seemed to faint away, he grew concerned and disturbed" (vol. 3, bk. XII, fol. 11v). The phrase contains three verbs referring to the state of Moteuczoma's heart. First, "it was as if his heart died" (*iuhquin iolmic*), a term often translated as fainting. Second "his heart was troubled" or afflicted (*moioltequipacho*), referring to pain and anxiety ([1571] Molina 1977: 105v [second numeration]; cf. Karttunen 1992: 232). Third, his heart was disturbed (*moiollacoma*) (39v [second numeration]). When the leader learned that the Spaniards desired to meet him, "to see his face," Moteuczoma experienced severe pain. The Nahuatl text employs two parallel expressions: *iuhquin patzmiquia yiollo* and *iolpatzmiquia*, which can be translated literally "as if his heart was killed by crushing or bruising," referring to his anguished state (Sahagún [1575–79] 1979: vol. 3, bk. XII, fol. 13v). The Nahua authors thus recorded that even before any physical interaction with Spaniards had occurred, the arrivals caused harm to the tlatoani.

As Moteuczoma learned about the powerful invaders, he attempted to send sickness, or *cocoliztli*, to the Spaniards. Instead of sending his best warriors to attack them, he assembled several formidable men, specialists who possessed magical powers to be used against the approaching Spaniards. The men sought to cast spells on the invaders "so that they would take sick [*cocolizcuique*], die, or turn back" (vol. 3, bk. XII, fol. 12v). The men returned from their mission, however, admitting "we are not their match; we are as nothing" (vol. 3, bk. XII, fol. 13). The powerful men lamented that the ability of the Spaniards to cause sickness and death far outmatched their own. When Moteuczoma heard that the men could not stop the invaders by inflicting sickness or death on them, he hoped to heal himself.

The health-threatening nature of Moteuczoma's malady is revealed in another part of Book XII, a chapter that describes his heart. Moteuczoma discussed his pain with those closest to him, his trusted advisors. He decided to search for a remedy by retreating to a purifying cave (vol. 3, bk. XII, fol. 14v). The cave retreat was a form of healing. The Nahuatl text confirmed its therapeutic nature. The purpose of the cave retreat was to find a cure (*inic vmpatiz*) (vol. 3, bk. XII, fol. 14v). The Nahuatl text used the verb *patia* meaning to cure or heal a sick person (Molina [1571] 1977: 80 [second numeration]; cf. Karttunen 1992: 184). His advisors were not able to help him find a remedy, however, and the leader braced himself for the approaching Spaniards.

In another instance, the Nahuatl text directly addressed the fright experienced by the leader. An additional set of messengers sent by Moteuczoma failed to meet the Spaniards and instead encountered a drunk Chalcan, the god Tezcatlipoca in disguise. In his translation Lockhart wrote that the deity ranted at the dumfounded group, and decrying the actions of Moteuczoma he asked, "Has he just now become a great coward?" (Lockhart 1993: 100–102). The question is translated by Anderson and Dibble as "Is he then perchance now overcome by a great fear?" ([1975] 2012: 33). The scholars translated the Nahuatl term *momauhticapul* differently as a combination of the verb *mauhtia* (having fear) (Molina [1571] 1977: 54 [second numeration]) with the preterit agentive (*-tica*) (the person carrying out the action of the verb) and the suffix *-pul* (big), which had derogatory connotations. Although the term coward is a valid translation, it does much to erase the condition of fear and adds a tone of blame. The Nahua authors of Book XII remembered a deeply troubled leader of Tenochtitlan. As Moteuczoma awaited the arrival of the Spaniards, he referred repeatedly to his ailing heart. But the Nahuatl text tells us that Moteuczoma eventually mastered his heart (*moiollotechiuh*) (Molina [1571] 1977: 92v [second numeration]). Two more phrases referred to Moteuczoma's heart and health before the arrival of the Spaniards. One phrase, *quioalcentlanqua in iiollo*, indicates that he managed to master his heart, in spite of his struggles. The descriptions of Moteuczoma's suffering heart draw attention to his failing health. But the Spanish translation of the Nahuatl text suggests weakness or cowardice, instead.

## Translating Nahua Cultural Concepts of Illness

Many sections of the Florentine Codex on health and the human body reveal a fundamental divergence between Nahua and Spanish concepts of illness. In the Nahuatl text of Book XII, during the initial stages of contact,

Moteuczoma "neither slept nor touched food. . . . He was tired and felt weak. He no longer found anything tasteful, enjoyable, or amusing" (Sahagún [1575–79] 1979: vol. 3, bk. XII, fol. 10). The Spanish column translates these conditions simply as sadness and fatigue "*sino estava muy triste . . . estava con grande congoxa*" (vol. 3, bk. XII, fol. 10). The Nahuatl describes symptoms of poor health that are translated into Spanish as a general state of weariness. The translation does not adequately explain the nature of his pain. The overlap between the different meanings attached to the word "heart" in European contexts often occludes what it may signal to Nahuas.

Nahuatl-language explanations of health and illness appear in metaphorical terms that often corresponded with physiological descriptions. Nahua authors used specific language to communicate ideas of physical and emotional states that were based on their cultural concepts of disease. Louise Burkhart's (1989: 99) research on the "Nahuatization" of Christian concepts in *The Slippery Earth* writes that "Christianity treated the symbolic relationship between physical and moral pollution primarily as metaphor, while Nahua ideology treated it primarily as metonym." Her research confirms that whereas Spaniards acknowledged a divide between physical and emotional/moral states, Nahuas believed in no such boundary. Nahua authors used physical and emotional descriptions to indicate the status of health of the human body. Therefore, in their descriptions of Moteuczoma's heart, the authors refer to a physical ailment.

Although Christian thought symbolically valued the heart, evidence from Nahua art reveals the importance of the organ independent of any interaction with Spanish friars. Several pre-Columbian statues display hearts, particularly stylized sacrificial hearts. In one famous statue of Coatlicue, the female deity wears a necklace composed of alternating hearts and human hands. The statue formed one part of a group of statues, according to Elizabeth Boone (1999: 192); another featured a figure wearing a skirt made entirely of human hearts. The statue, commonly called Yolotlicue (her skirt is hearts), represented a powerful woman goddess who, along with several other women, sacrificed themselves to light and heat the world. In her examination of the Coatlicue statue, Cecelia Klein (2008: 233) clarifies that it represented an "important creator goddess who along with several other deities (all of whom, according to one source, were likewise female) long ago gave up their lives to give birth to and energize the fifth and present sun." Klein (237) draws attention to the form and red color of the tuna nopal cactus fruit and how the Aztecs associated it with the human heart. The links between the human heart, light, energy, and life itself are vested in the symbolic and figural representations found in the

Yolotlicue and Coatlicue statues. The importance of the heart for heat and life is found in pre-contact forms of sacrifice and a postcontact focus on the heart as an indicator of life and health.

Several sections of the Florentine Codex reveal the importance of the heart in the memories of colonial Nahuas. The heart was an important sacrifice during the ceremony of Tlacaxipeualiztli. In one part of the ceremony, the Nahua removed the hearts of captives to make offerings to the sun and the eagle. The Nahua priests called the human hearts "precious-eagle-cactus-fruit," explaining their important status (Sahagún [1575–79] 1979: vol. I, bk. II, f. 18v).[4] The heart represented a treasured life-sustaining thing, the ultimate offering from human beings. In making offerings to the Mexica patron god Huitzilopochtli, priests formed the god's body from amaranth dough and then ate the body, reserving the heart for Moteuczoma (Sahagún [1575–79] 1979: vol. I, bk. III, fol. 4v). The descriptions of hearts in connection with the fates of humans, their personalities, and their emotions in Book IV exemplify it as the signifier of personal volition (Sahagún [1575–79] 1979: vol. I, bk. IV, fols. 14–44). Similarly, descriptions of vices and virtues in Book X consistently refer to a person's heart as the seat of their disposition and health. For example, the lewd youth who was very sick was called a person who lost his heart or had an evil heart (Sahagún [1575–79] 1979: vol. 3, bk. X, fol. 24v). Clearly, the heart served as a vital bodily organ and a moral compass. The Nahuas likely viewed the heart as the seat of a life force, as evidenced by the pre-Columbian iconography and their ceremonies that continued during the colonial period.

Nahuas living during the colonial period may have easily identified their understanding of the heart with the Spanish concept of the human soul. Molina defined the soul with the Nahuatl terms *teyolia* and *teyolitia* (Molina [1571] 1977: 8v [first numeration]). Molina also supplied the Spanish-language loanword for soul, *anima*, with the Nahuatl *te-* prefix: *teanima*. The same definition appears in the Nahuatl-language section of the dictionary. Removing the indefinite possessive prefix *te-*, the Nahuatl section of the dictionary defines *yoli* as a living thing (39v [second numeration]). As a verb, *yoli* signified "to live, revive, or incubate an egg," definitions that reinforce a general sense of life. A related noun, *yollotli*, is defined as the heart, linking Nahua ideas of a life force to a physical bodily location (41). Alfredo López Austin (1984: 252–57) observed that the human heart was the seat of the life force of the *teyolia*. According to Frances E. Karttunen (1992: 340), author of the modern analytical dictionary of Nahuatl based on several sixteenth-century sources, the prefix *yol-* indicates "an extended sense that encompasses emotion, volition, strength, valor, and heart." When Nahuas used the prefix *yol-* they indicated a thing's physical and spiritual elements. The repeated references to Moteuczoma's heart indicated his physical and spiritual ailment.

The Nahua authors of the Florentine Codex consulted with sixteen different Nahua healers to create the sections that describe the functions of the human body and cures for ailments (Sahagún [1575–79] 1979: vol. 3, bk. X, fol. 113v; fol. 106). In the text they created, they described the heart as round and hot, "that by which there is life, it makes one live . . . it sustains one" (Sahagún [1575–79] 1979: vol. 3, bk. X, fol. 91v). A section focused on body organs described heart death or *njiolmjquj*. Molina defined the suffering of heart death as "to faint, die away, have unease/itch, or to be frightened" (Molina [1571] 1977: 41 [second numeration]). Nahuas used descriptions of heart afflictions to indicate poor health. Fright was a common cause for heart afflictions. Fright had severe physical and spiritual consequences that affected the heart, long-term health, and the emotional well-being of the victim. In the definition for the term *mauhcatlacayotl* or cowardice—*covuardia*—Molina adds that it also could be defined as a lack of spirit or *falta de animo* (Molina [1571] 1977: 54 [second numeration]). Evidence from colonial and contemporary sources reveals heart-death from fright as a long-standing Mesoamerican concept of illness.

## Heart-Death and Fright in Colonial Herbals

Nahuas writing in the sixteenth century considered fright an illness, evident from its listing as a type of illness in two herbals from the colonial era. Colonial sources on herbal remedies confirm that fear required treatment. One herbal, known as the *Cruz-Badiano Codex*, written in 1552 by indigenous physicians and scribes, documents indigenous plants and their medicinal uses (Badiano, Cruz, Treviño [1552] 2008). Martín de la Cruz, a Nahua physician, composed an illustrated herbal in association with colleagues at the College of Santa Cruz, Tlatelolco. Intended for King Carlos I of Spain, the herbal was translated into Latin by another Nahua scholar, Juan Badiano. Each page of the codex is illustrated with images of plants, whereas the text describes the therapeutic qualities of plants, animals, and minerals. The text documents many bicultural concepts of health but also several distinctly Nahua cultural concepts such as a description of fright illness (Gimmel 2008: 169–92).

The *Cruz-Badiano* dedicated an entire page to remedies for the illness of fright. The remedy for fright appears after the remedy for warts and before a section on eliminating armpit stench, a placement suggesting the mundane nature of fright illness. The text recommended an herbal concoction of *tonatiuh-yxiuh*, *tlanextia-yxiuh*, and *tetlahuitl* along with the flowers of the *cacalo-xochitl*, *cacaua-xochitl*, and *tzacouh-xochitl* and a poultice made with several more ingredients. The text, in Latin, explained that the cure was appropriate for a person who had fright or was "fear-burdened" (Badiano, Cruz, Treviño [1552] 2008: fol. 53). Two images of herbs are drawn above with Nahuatl-language labels that correspond to one of the herbs mentioned in the recipe. The remedies prescribed in the *Cruz-Badiano* offer material solutions to what the Nahua considered a physical and spiritual affliction.

The herbal section of the Florentine Codex found in Book XI confirms the link between fright and illness. One section on healing plants lists an herbal remedy for someone suffering from certain conditions of fright. The text recommends a treatment made from the herb *oquichpatli* to treat a person who had been frightened during sex and suffered from the experience. The text states that "even if she or he has been sick already one year, or even already four years, [treatment] is required" (Sahagún [1575–79] 1979: vol. 3, bk. XII, fol. 173). Such information reinforces the long-term illness associated with fright, a characteristic unique to Nahua cultural concepts of illness.

### Fright beyond Moteuczoma in Book XII

The tendency to blame Moteuczoma does not account for the fact that regular Nahuas also suffered similar symptoms during the invasion of their altepetl. The common people depicted in Book XII also experienced fright and poor health. For example, when the messengers rushed back to Tenochtitlan, they described their news as very terrifying or *cenca tema-mauhti* (Sahagún [1575–79] 1979: vol. 3, bk. XII, fol. 10). Accurately, Molina's *Vocabulario* ([1571] 1977: 97 [second numeration]) defines *temamauhti* as a frightening or fearful thing. However, consider how a similar entry on the same page, the noun *temauh*, is relevant here: *temauh* is defined as an infectious thing, something that gives sickness to others. The following entry, *temauh cocoliztli*, refers to contagious sickness. After these two words related to disease, the *Vocabulario* lists *temauhti* as something that scares or puts fear into others. These nouns come from two different verb roots that share the same form in the preterit tense, *omauh* (97). The similarities between the words suggests a direct connection between fear and illness in Mesoamerican culture. The polluting consequences of the frightful encounter destroyed the leader's health and, ultimately, the health of his people.

The health of the Nahua leaders was thought to have a direct impact on the welfare of their people. Miguel Pastrana Flores has noted how the failures or bad behaviors of leaders could leave the city in grave danger (Pastrana Flores 2004: 133–5). Book VI of the Florentine Codex, on rhetoric and philosophy, confirms this connection with two adages linking the health of the leader to the condition of his people. One proverb admonished the rulers to ignore their suffering and eat well because "anguish will become a grave sickness" (Sahagún [1575–79] 1979: vol. 2, bk. VI, fol. 210). Another described the results of a bad leader's behavior as pain, sickness, or famine. It likened the punishment of sickness to the leader throwing cold water on the people. This connection between the health of the tlatoani and the condition of his people sheds light on how the authors of Book XII imagined Moteuczoma's health in light of the welfare of his people. The Nahua authors connected the health and comportment of the leader with the well-being of the common people.

The idea of Moteuczoma as a scapegoat does not adequately explain the fact that the Nahua authors of Book XII also describe the common people as debilitated by fear. The Nahua authors of Book XII explained the imminent health disaster by focusing on the conditions of fright in the altepetl. In the introduction to his translation of Book XII, Lockhart (1993: 5) objected to scholars who concluded that the Nahua were "a people shocked out of its senses, amazed, bewildered, overwhelmed, benumbed by intruders, paralyzed, fate-ridden, prepared for imminent doom and disappearance." Lockhart qualified his disbelief in the image of the cowardly Nahuas by admitting that it is not possible to consult immediate postconquest Nahuatl documents. I argue that the fright documented in Book XII should be considered an early symptom of the diseases that would devastate Tenochtitlan a year later, in 1520.

It was not only the leader who suffered. When Moteuczoma processed the news about the new threat to his altepetl, he began to weep. According to the text, when the leader suffered his people suffered too, found in Book XII as "he told the troubles of the altepetl" (Sahagún [1575–79] 1979: vol. 3, bk. XII, fol. 13). At that point, everyone experienced tremendous fright. During that time "fear reigned, and shock, laments, and expressions of distress" prevailed (Sahagún [1575–79] 1979: vol. 3, bk. XII, fol. 13v). Even the enemies of the Mexica, the Tlaxcalans, endured the oppressive fright inspired by the Spaniards. When the Tlaxcalans heard about the massacres committed by Spaniards as they marched inland, the Nahuatl text explains, "they became limp with fear, they were made to faint, and fear took hold of them" (Sahagún [1575–79] 1979: vol. 3, bk. XII, fol. 15). The Tlaxcalans, weakened with sickening fright, decided to ally themselves with the Spaniards, perhaps to avoid the massacre of their own people.

The fright of the Mexica people intensified after the first meeting between Moteuczoma and Cortés, despite the calm words spoken. The text recounts that the Spaniards entreated the Nahua leader to "be at ease, let him not be afraid" (Sahagún [1575–79] 1979: vol. 3, bk. XII, fol. 26). The phrase for being at ease is *ma moiollali*, which can be translated literally as "let his heart be composed" (Molina [1571] 1977: 40r, 40v, 124 [second numeration]). The people also suffered heart pains when the Spaniards took their leader captive and occupied his palace. Once again, the people witnessed a major upheaval of the natural order. It was a time when "everything became confused. . . . Fear reigned, as though everyone had swallowed his heart . . . everyone was terrified, taken aback, thunderstruck, stunned" (Sahagún [1575–79] 1979: vol. 3, bk. XII, fol. 11). The Spanish translation adds another interesting layer to the intense nature of fear, stating that "both those present and those absent conceived a mortal fright (Sahagún [1575–79] 1979: vol. 3, bk. XII, fol. 11).The fright was not confined to those who witnessed Moteuczoma being taken captive. The fear spread to all the people of the altepetl. The Nahuatl text includes everyone in their descriptions; these descriptions of widespread fear sound more like an infectious disease rather than an emotional affliction.

The text takes pains to point out the infectious nature of the fright. As the Spaniards looted the palace and demanded food, the Nahuas continued to suffer. During Moteuczoma's captivity "Fear greatly prevailed; it spread about" (Sahagún [1575–79] 1979: vol. 3, bk. XII, fol. 29; (Molina [1571] 1977: 106 [second numeration]). The Nahuatl phrase contains another facet of the fear during the time of the conquest. In the phrase for "it spread about," *mauiztli moteteca*, the first term, *mauiztli*, means fear or something worthy of respect or awe (Molina [1571] 1977: 54v [second numeration]). The noun sheds light on another element of terror for Nahuas writing in the sixteenth century: fear always existed in relation to respect. They knew that anything worthy of marvel and respect was also a force to be feared. The fear invoked by the actions of the Spaniards spread the fright illness from the Mexica leader to his people. These precipitating terrifying events were perhaps how the Nahua authors explained the impending disease epidemics.

### Fright Illness and the First Disease Epidemic

The chapter in Book XII that describes the first epidemic comes after the expulsion of the Spaniards from the city but before the Spaniards remount an attack. The Nahuatl text explains "before the Spaniards appeared to us, first an epidemic broke out, a sickness of pustules" (Sahagún [1575–79]

1979: vol. 3, bk. XII, fol. 53v). The authors identified the sickness of pustules as *cocoliztli totomonaliztli*. The noun *cocoliztli* conveyed a meaning that is not represented in Spanish words for disease. For the Nahua authors, *cocoliztli* signified a major social disruption or great pain. Molina's *Vocabulario* defined *cocoliztli* simply as sickness. But in a Mesoamerican world devoid of widespread epidemic diseases, I infer that the word had a meaning closer to the verb on which it is based, *cocoa*. Molina defined *cocoa* in different ways, depending on its prefix, as being hurt or sick, and when transitive, to hurt another person. Karttunen (1992: 38) acknowledged the intersection of meaning between hurt and sickness. In an attempt to address the separate entries with similar meanings, she includes under the entry for *cocoa*, "the sense of 'to be sick' may arise from confusion with *cocoy(a)*, or it may derive from the shared sense of pain." The applicative form of the verb, *cocolia*, means to "hate or wish someone ill" (Molina [1571] 1977: 23v [second numeration]). The term possesses a semantic range from physical disease to hatred, suggesting that Nahua concepts of illness and hatred are much the same.

In contrast to the Spanish terms *viruela* or *pestilencia*, the Nahuatl term for disease, *cocoliztli*, indicated the social conditions of disaster, along with the physical suffering from disease. The text explains that the "pustules that covered people caused great desolation; very many people died of them" (Sahagún [1575–79] 1979: vol. 3, bk. XII, fol. 53v). The result of the diseases was written succinctly in the Nahuatl column. It reported that due to *cocoliztli* many indigenous people died: "many local people died" (Sahagún [1575–79] 1979: vol. 3, bk. XII, fol. 53).The Nahuatl column carefully denoted that the disease afflicted indigenous people, but not the Spaniards, with the phrase "*nican tlaca*." Lockhart (1993: 13) translated this phrase as "here people," one of the only Nahua terms in the text that "indicated the local, native inhabitants of central Mexico." The authors recognized that the first epidemic disease largely affected indigenous communities.

The negative social aspects associated with *cocoliztli* are clear when comparing it to other words used for disease. These terms have meanings clearly related to the physical appearance of lumps or swelling of sections of skin. Many of the Nahuatl words for disease were descriptive terms lacking broader meanings. For example, *totomoniliztli* is a noun that refers to pustules or blisters (Molina [1571] 1977: 150v [second numeration]). Another common noun was the word *zahuatl*, pox or rash (Siméon 2010: 71; Karttunen 1992: 345). The words describing the physical symptoms were often used in combination with *cocoliztli*, indicating that widespread deadly disease consisted of more than bumps on the skin.

The noun based on the verb *cocoa*, *cocoliztli* refers to widespread pain, including all types of hatred and suffering. The explanations of harmful acts causing suffering found in the Florentine Codex reveal the moral judgment of the authors. Burkhart argues that "moral discourse operated not on the assumption that acts had polluting effects but on the assumption that the pollution resulting obviously and directly from the act would bring with it a host of other nasty effects" (Burkhart 1989: 99). The Nahua authors of Book XII documented social disruptions in their choice of language; they chose to describe the first epidemic with the term *cocoliztli*.

In their discussion of the consequences of the epidemic disease, the Nahuatl text confirms that "the Mexica warriors were greatly weakened by it" (Sahagún [1575–79] 1979: vol. 3, bk. XII, fol. 54). Here, the Nahua authors make an explicit connection between the debilitating diseases and their ability to defend their city. The translation matches the Nahuatl nearly word for word until the last sentence about the weakened warriors. Ironically, the final sentence of the Spanish-language column remarks that the Nahua "resisted them strongly" (Sahagún [1575–79] 1979: vol. 3, bk. XII, fol. 53v). Of these radically different versions of events, scholars have largely relied on the Spanish-language version. Only by examining the Nahuatl-language text and delving into the cultural concepts of disease of the Nahua scholars and elders who wrote Book XII can we analyze their perspective. Disease, heart afflictions, fright, and the conquest must have been intertwined in the minds of the authors of Book XII.

Although this analysis of Nahuatl disease terminology in colonial-era *vocabularios* and herbals illustrates how Nahuas may have thought of fright illness, more illuminating information can be found in modern ethnographic studies. Native Nahuatl speakers today continue to refer to the heart as essential to the living nature of a being. For example, in their dictionary, Nahuatl speakers from the Huasteca in Veracruz refer to a person's health in their first example listed under the term *yollotl*, "heart" (Sullivan et al. 2016: 613). Modern-day Nahuatl speakers continue to consider the health-threatening nature of fright illness and its long-term effects.

### Soul Loss, Fright Illness, or *Susto* in Modern Ethnographic Studies

Both colonial and modern sources regard fright to be an illness with long-term implications and cite a similar set of symptoms. Modern ethnographic research has documented the symptoms of and treatments for fright illness often referred to as *susto*. Several studies in medical anthropology recognize susto in Mexico. In their research on communities in southern Mexico, anthropologists find susto to be a widely known concept with a well-established etiology, diagnosis, and regimen of healing. The research of Arthur J. Rubel, Carl W. O'nell, and Rolando Collado-Ardón (1984: 43) shows that although "the element of fright . . . is always present in the people's account of events to which susto is attributed, probing uncovers that it is not the fright itself" that creates the long-term suffering of the individual. Similarly, while working with the Nahuatl-speaking peoples of the Huasteca, Alan Sandstrom (1991: 301) confirms that Nahua medicine "tends to look for the ultimate causes or conditions that led that particular patient's body to become vulnerable to disease in the first place." Thus, according to modern research, Nahuas related the origin of many forms of illness referred to as susto to a frightening experience.

Indigenous people of the Americas, especially in Mexico, associate fright with subsequent illness. In most cases, the precipitating event or fright experience occurs independently; it could be separated by weeks or years from the onset of symptoms or eventual illness. In a study among the Zapotecs of Oaxaca, Carl O'nell (1975: 52) found that "most susto experiences are characterized by a period of considerable delay between attributed fright and the emergence of the symptoms of the illness." Most studies mark a clear separation between the frightening event and the full-blown appearance of a pathological disease. These findings may explain why the Nahua authors of Book XII chose to describe the experiences of the messengers and Moteuczoma long before they described the onset of the first epidemic.

Although the Florentine Codex was written long before modern studies, the symptoms of susto are strikingly similar. In one study based on work with Spanish-speaking populations, Janice Klein (1978: 23) summarizes that in the examined cases of susto, there is a "common thread of helplessness and inability to act and remove the cause of the fear." Symptoms include restlessness, lack of sleep, listlessness, loss of appetite, and depression.

The frightening experience, or the cause of susto, held severe consequences for long-term bodily and spiritual health. Proceeding from the accepted definition of *susto* as "soul loss through magical fright or simply fright," the anthropologist Avisi Mysyk (1998: 187) directly links the suffering from fright to a form of the soul. I argue it could be the vital force associated with the heart. Loss of a person's vital force due to fright caused illness far beyond the initial frightening event. The Spanish term for soul, *ánima*, is a poor translation for what indigenous groups considered to be the vital forces of the body. In Sandstrom's words (1989: 357), the Nahua pantheistic worldview considers that "the universe itself is a sacred, indivisible whole and everything in it is an aspect of deity. All things, including human beings, plants, and everyday objects have a spirit presence. . . . " It is impossible to divide intangible life forces from the material world. One early study made a distinction between how people of different cultural backgrounds interpreted the cause of susto. Arthur J. Rubel (1964) found that people from indigenous groups stressed that soul loss was caused by contact with supernatural beings, whereas people with mestizo backgrounds diagnose soul loss as caused by a fright. That soul loss and/or fright ailments continue to be found in research among Spanish-speaking populations in the United States demonstrates the long-term relevance of the illness.

### Susto, or Fright Illness, as Understood by US Medical Practitioners

Medical doctors are asked to understand folk illnesses such as *susto*, which can be found in Mexican and Mexican American culture, highlighting the enduring remnants of a non-Western medical culture. They are encouraged to practice cross-cultural medicine; during their time with a patient they "should elicit the patient's perception of the illness and any alternative therapies he or she is undergoing as well as facilitate a mutually acceptable treatment plan" (Juckett 2005: 2267). Patients' perceptions of illness and cultural concepts of disease remain important for researchers today, although some authors prefer the phrases "culture-bound syndromes" or "folk illness"—that is, a combination of psychiatric and somatic symptoms that are considered to be a recognizable disease only within a specific society or culture (Simons and Hughes 1985; Ortiz de Montellano 1989: 3). For Latino or Hispanic patients, one research article encourages, health care providers should "consider discussing these illnesses in a non-judgmental manner with patients who present with symptoms that are consistent with these syndromes" (Bayles and Katerndahl 2009: 28). Today, US doctors can take courses focused on lay health beliefs or read articles on folk illnesses that are part of cultural heritage.

Significantly, English-language articles on the phenomenon of fright illness retain the Spanish term susto. Several recent authors maintain the Spanish term even in the titles of their articles, revealing it to be a well-recognized affliction (Durà-Vilà and Hodes 2012; Weller et al. 2008; Mendenhall et al. 2012). In other words, modern medical researchers choose not to translate from Spanish to English an illness that at one time was found primarily among the indigenous inhabitants of Latin America. Their findings attribute susto to a set of standard biomedical conditions. Some link it to depressive disorders, others to a somatoform disorder [a category of mental disorder], and still others to hypoglycemia. In his 2005 article on cross-cultural medicine, Dr. Gregory Juckett (2005: 2270) places susto in a list of traditional Latino diagnoses. He explains it consists of fright-induced "soul loss," which he diagnoses as post-traumatic illness (e.g., shock, insomnia, depression, anxiety). He continues that the traditional treatment for the illness is a sweeping purification or *barrida* ceremony (that is repeated until the patient improves). In his study of cleansing ceremonies in Mexico, Alfonso Julio Aparicio Mena (2009: 5) records that according to the people he consulted that "being upset can cause susto. A cleansing is necessary to unblock the consequences of the emotion." Mena's research links the importance of the cleansing treatment for susto that resonates with scenes of the codex. The descriptions of cleansing recall the ceremony performed on Moteuczoma in Book XII, when he suffered his first heart and fright afflictions. In his description of the sweeping purification ceremony, Dr. Juckett identifies an illness unique to Mexican and Mexican American populations and explains a cleansing ritual to an audience of American doctors who seek to communicate better with their patients.

In his attempt to characterize a distinctly Mesoamerican illness, Dr. Juckett paid little attention to how Latinos themselves define susto. Latinos define susto radically different than depression, much like Nahuas defined fright radically different than cowardice. In their study of susto, Megan Lemly and Lori A. Spies (2015) find that Latinos associate it with another type of illness: type II diabetes. Several symptoms of type II diabetes include irritability and fatigue, symptoms that are consistent with descriptions of susto in Book XII. Conducting research with Mexican American inhabitants of the US-Mexico borderlands, Jane Poss and Mary Ann Jezewski (2002: 368) found that "nearly all of the participants could pinpoint a specific episode of fright (which they termed susto) or a profound emotional experience as the contributing factor in the development of their own diabetes." In their 2016 article on the causes that Spanish-speaking patients attribute to diabetes, Dr. Jeannie B. Concha et al. (2016) explain that understanding cultural diabetes causation beliefs such as susto can improve communication with Hispanic/Latino patients. The gulf between what some diagnose as a psychiatric disorder to type II diabetes reveals that when we pay close attention to how people in a cultural community define illness, we arrive at profoundly different conclusions about the nature of an ailment.

Apart from sweeping ceremonies, the cures found in the research of Lemly and Spies include the herbal remedies of *sabila* (aloe vera) and *nopal* (prickly pear cactus), two products widely used in Mesoamerica. The authors call attention to research that confirms the efficacy of the plants in lowering sugar levels. The authors' attention to traditional methods of curing encourages a bicultural understanding of healing methods. The authors continue to argue that awareness about "susto beliefs . . . and development of culturally sensitive communication skills are essential for nurse practitioners to effectively assist patients in this population to achieve their glycemic goals" (Lemly and Spies 2015: 185). These research articles claim that medical professionals are more effective when they blend cultural understanding and medical research. Their research on susto, an illness with undeniable roots in Mesoamerican indigenous cultures, speaks to the cultural longevity of Mesoamerican cultural concepts of illness in Mexico and the United States.

Medical sources from colonial and contemporary times present a clear picture of the cultural concept of susto. It is a condition often but not always linked to soul loss and causes long-term suffering. Precipitated by a terrifying experience, it causes the victim to withdraw from normal activities and cease to function in society. Although Western doctors often link it with mood disorders such as depression, Mexicans, Mexicans with indigenous origins, Mexican Americans, and Latinos cite it as the cause for the long-term bodily illness of diabetes. Although we may never determine how Nahuas conceived of the soul, the heart seems a likely candidate for the vehicle of a life-giving force. The Nahua authors of Book XII indicated that Moteuczoma suffered from susto, not cowardice.

## Conclusions

This article reinterprets the memories of Moteuczoma Xocoyotzin's leadership with the use of Nahua cultural concepts of illness. I argue that the leader suffered from fright illness, an ailment defined in colonial sources that survives as the etiological entity susto in modern indigenous communities. By recognizing that Moteuczoma suffered from illness rather than cowardice, we can understand how the Nahua authors of the Florentine Codex remembered their huei tlatoani and, by extension, the reaction of their community to the invasion and subsequent epidemics.

The Nahuatl text in Book XII of the Florentine Codex repeatedly refers to fright and heart afflictions in descriptions of Moteuczoma. Nahuas recounting history in the sixteenth century did not distinguish between physical and emotional ailments. For many Nahua, the heart was an organ that influenced physical and emotional health. It had the power to sustain life and affect the fate or general state of the person, as something akin to a soul. The unpredictable and violent acts perpetrated by the Spaniards traumatized Moteuczoma, but he suffered alongside his people.

The broader Nahua community experienced severe fright at the news and actions of the Spaniards. Poor health spread easily from the leader to his people during the turbulent events of the conquest. Much like their leader, the illness experienced by the common people was expressed in fright and heart afflictions. The complicated nature of how Nahuas understood the bodily implications of fright, soul loss, and heart-related afflictions was partially documented in colonial herbals. Modern ethnographic studies add to our understanding of culture-bound syndromes.

Descriptions of heart afflictions and fright in the text of Book XII closely mirror symptoms of fright illness or susto found in contemporary ethnographic accounts. Although diagnosis and treatments have changed for traditional healers and doctors since the colonial period, a comparison between colonial and modern evidence reveals the widespread acknowledgement of the susto illness and its long-term effects. People living in modern indigenous communities and Nahuas writing during the colonial period described afflictions quite distinct from the morally fraught condition of cowardice.

Cultural concepts of illness were often lost in the translation from Nahuatl to Spanish in the codex. The differences between the texts reveal that Nahua concepts were translated into Spanish as fear or anxiety. Also, the varied definitions of the general term for illness, *cocoliztli*, represent diverse notions of disease that are not found in the Spanish translation of the Book XII. Even the various methods for translating fear-related terms from the Nahuatl text are informed by Western notions of emotions. Instead of blaming their leader, the Nahua authors logically focused on representing their cultural concepts of illness, because they remembered the devastating impact of the first epidemic during the invasion and the subsequent waves of disease as they composed drafts of the codex.

It is not coincidental that the Nahua authors distinctly remembered fright illness introduced by the Spaniards as a prelude to the epidemics that swept through their communities. Nahuas relied on their cultural concepts of health and illness to understand the conquest's destruction, in which disease was a major factor. They may have thought of disease and conquest as one and the same. Clearly, disease directly impacted the health of the Mexica and debilitated its traditional defenses. Nahuas who survived the colonial period wrote about illness in ways we have yet to decipher according to their own concepts of illness. Only through an understanding of Nahua concepts of illness can we begin to glimpse their perception of the Spanish-led invasion and widespread epidemic diseases that afflicted their communities in the sixteenth century.

Building on this work, future research on Moteuczoma's suffering during the conquest should interrogate notions of masculinity and how they inform judgment of the leader. Future research should reconsider gendered responsibilities in the face of violence and their connections to Western ideas of cowardice. Especially helpful is what James M. Taggart called "relational masculinity" in his ethnography of Nahua oral narrations and cultural traditions. In this conception of masculinity, "a man should act carefully lest he disrupt the fragile order of his body, his family, and his cosmos" (1997: 243). Remembering Moteuczoma's actions as careful and not cowardly, especially considering that his body, family, and cosmos were under threat, would aid the continued reinterpretation of the leader's role during the conquest.

## Notes

I would like to thank Kevin Terraciano, Louise Burkhart, John Schwaller, Kim Richter, Pamela Munro, Mary Terrall, Sabina Cruz de la Cruz, Kathryn Renton, and the anonymous reviewers from *Ethnohistory* for their support and time dedicated to improving my research.

1   For more on ethnographic upstreaming and downstreaming, see Fenton 1962; Axtell 1979; White 1991; Galloway 2006.
2   See Anderson and Dibble 1950–82 for a full history of the twelve books of the Florentine Codex.
3   Lockhart (1993: 20) explained that we are still very far from understanding the true meaning of "god," or *teotl* in Nahuatl.
4   An image of an eagle eating the sacrificial heart held aloft by a priest is found in Book XI: Sahagún (1575–79) 1979 vol. 3, bk. XI, fol. 47v.

## References

Acuna-Soto, Rene, David W. Stahle, Malocom K. Cleaveland, and Mathew D. Therrell, 2002. "Megadrought and Megadeath in Sixteenth-Century Mexico." *Emerging Infectious Disease* 8, no. 4: 360–62.
Anderson, Arthur J. O., and Charles E. Dibble, trans. [1975] 2012. *Book 12 — The Conquest of Mexico* of *Florentine Codex: General History of the Things of New Spain*. 13 vols. Santa Fe, NM: School of American Research and the University of Utah Press.
Anderson, Arthur J. O., and Charles E. Dibble, trans. [1982] 2012. *Introduction and Indices* of *Florentine Codex: General History of the Things of New Spain*. 13 vols. Santa Fe, NM: School of American Research and the University of Utah Press.
Aparicio Mena, Alfonso Julio. 2009. "La Limpia en las etnomedicinas mesoamericanas." *Gazeta de Antropología* 25, no. 1. hdl.handle.net/10481/54702.

Axtell, James. 1979. "Ethnohistory: An Historian's Viewpoint." *Ethnohistory* 26, no. 1: 1–13.

Badiano, Juan, and Martín de la Cruz. [1552] 2008. *Codice de la Cruz-Badiano.* Serie Códices de México 7. Carlos Viesca Treviño, ed. Mexico City: Consejo Nacional para la Cultura y las Artes and The National Institute of Anthropology and History.

Bayles, Bryan P., David A. Katerndahl. 2009. "Culture-Bound Syndromes in Hispanic Primary Care Patients." *International Journal of Psychiatry in Medicine*, May 22.

Boone, Elizabeth H. 1999. "The 'Coatlicues' at the Templo Mayor." *Ancient Mesoamerica* 10, no. 2: 189–206.

Burkhart, Louise. 1989. *The Slippery Earth: Nahua-Christian Moral Dialogue in Sixteenth-Century Mexico.* Tucson: University of Arizona Press.

Concha, Jeannie B., Sallie D. Mayer, Briana R. Mezuk, and Danielle Avula. 2016. "Diabetes Causation Beliefs among Spanish-Speaking Patients." *Diabetes Education* 42, no. 1: 116–25.

Cook, Sherburne Friend, and Lesley Byrd Simpson. 1948. *Ibero Americana* 31. Berkeley: University of California Press.

Cook, Sherburne F., and Woodrow Borah. 1957. "The Rate of Population Change in Central México 1550–1570." *Hispanic American Historical Review* 37, no. 4: 463–70.

Cuadriello, Jaime. 2009. "Moctezuma Through the Centuries." In *Race and Classification: The Case of Mexican America*, edited by Illona Katzew and Susan Deans-Smith. Stanford, CA: Stanford University Press, 119–150.

Durà-Vilà, Gloria, and Mathew Hodes. 2012. "Cross-Cultural Study of Idioms of Distress among Spanish Nationals and Hispanic American Migrants: Susto, Nervios, and Ataque de Nervios." *Social Psychiatry and Psychiatry Epidemiology* 47, no. 10: 1627–37.

Fenton, William. 1962. "Ethnohistory and Its Problems." *Ethnohistory* 9, no. 1: 1–23.

Few, Martha. 2008. "Indian Autopsy and Epidemic Disease in Early Colonial Mexico." In *Invasion and Transformation: Interdisciplinary Perspectives on the Conquest of Mexico*, edited by Rebecca Parker Brienen and Margaret A. Jackson, 153–66. Boulder: University Press of Colorado.

Galloway, Patricia. 2006. *Practicing Ethnohistory: Mining Archives, Hearing Testimony, Constructing Narratives.* Lincoln: University of Nebraska Press.

Gibson, Charles. 1964. *The Aztecs under Spanish Rule: A History of the Indians of the Valley of Mexico.* Stanford, CA: Stanford University Press.

Gillespie, Susan D. 2008. "Blaming Moteuczoma: Anthropomorphizing the Aztec Conquest" in *Invasion and Transformation: Interdisciplinary Perspectives on the Conquest of Mexico*, edited by Rebecca Parker Brienen and Margaret A. Jackson, 25–56. Boulder: University Press of Colorado.

Gimmel, Millie. 2008. "Reading Medicine in the Codex de la Cruz Badiano." *Journal of the History of Ideas* 69, no. 2: 169–92.

Huber, Brad R., and Alan R. Sandstrom. 2001. *Mesoamerican Healers.* Austin: University of Texas Press.

Juckett, Gregory. 2005. "Cross-Cultural Medicine." *American Family Physician.* 72, no. 11: 2267–74.

Karttunen, Frances E. 1992. *An Analytical Dictionary of Nahuatl.* Norman: University of Oklahoma Press.

Klein, Cecelia F. 2008. "A New Interpretation of the Aztec Statue Called Coatlicue, 'Snakes-Her-Skirt.'" *Ethnohistory* 55, no. 2: 229–50.

Klein, Janice. 1978. "*Susto*: The Anthropological Study of Diseases of Adaptation." *Social Science and Medicine* 12: 23–28.

Lemley, Megan, and Lori A. Spies. 2015. "Traditional Beliefs and Practices among Mexican American Immigrants with Type II Diabetes: A Case Study." *Journal of American Association of Nurse Practitioners* 27, no. 4: 185–89.

Lockhart, James, ed. and trans. 1993. *We People Here: Nahuatl Accounts of the Conquest of Mexico.* Berkeley: University of California Press.

López Austin, Alfredo. 1984. *Cuerpo humano e ideología: Las concepciones de los antiguos nahuas.* Mexico City: Universidad Nacional Autónoma de México, Instituto de Investigaciones Antropológicas.

Mendenhall, Emily, Alicia Fernandez, Nancy Adler, and Elizabeth A. Jacobs. 2012. "Susto, Coraje, and Abuse: Depression and Beliefs about Diabetes." *Culture, Medicine and Psychiatry* 36, no. 3: 480–92.

Molina, Alonso de. (1571) 1977. *Vocabulario en lengua castellana y mexicana y mexicana y castellana.* Mexico City: Editorial Porrúa.

Mysyk, Avisi. 1998. "Susto: An Illness of the Poor." *Dialectical Anthropology.* Vol. 23, no. 2:187–202.

O'nell, Carl. 1975. "An Investigation of Reported 'Fright' as a Factor in the Etiology of Susto, 'Magical Fright.'" *Ethos*3, no. 1: 41–63.

Ortiz de Montellano, Bernard. 1989. *Syncretism in Mexican and Mexican-American Folk Medicine.* College Park: University of Maryland at College Park.

Pastrana Flores, Miguel. 2004. *Historias de la Conquista: Aspectos de la historiografía de tradición náhuatl.* Mexico City: Universidad Nacional Autónoma de México.

Poss, Jane, and Mary Ann Jezewski. 2002. "The Role and Meaning of Susto in Mexican Americans' Explanatory Model of Type 2 Diabetes." *Medical Anthropology Quarterly* 16, no. 3: 360–77.

Prescott, William. 1891. *History of the Conquest of Mexico.* London: Swan Sonnenschein.

Restall, Matthew. 2018. *When Montezuma Met Cortés: The True Story of the Meeting that Changed History.* New York: Ecco.

Rubel, Arthur J. 1965. "The Epidemiology of a Folk Illness: *Susto* in Hispanic America." *Ethonology* 3: 268–83.

Rubel, Arthur J., Carl W. O'Nell, and Rolando Collado-Ardón. 1984. *Susto: A Folk Illness.* Berkeley: University of California Press.

Sahagún, Bernardino de. (1575–79) 1979. *Códice florentino.* Mexico City: Secretaría de Gobernación.

Sandstrom, Alan. 1989. "The Face of the Devil: Concepts of Disease and Pollution among Nahua Indians of the Southern Huasteca." *Enquêtes sur l'Amérique moyenne: Mélanges offerts à Guy Stresser-Péan*, edited by Guy Stresser-Péan and Dominique Michelet, 357–73. Mexico City: Instituto Nacional de Antropología e Historia, Consejo Nacional para la Cultura y las Artes, and Centre d'études mexicaines et centraméricaines.

Sandstrom, Alan. 1991. *Corn Is Our Blood: Culture and Ethnic Identity in a Contemporary Aztec Indian Village*. Norman: University of Oklahoma Press.

Siméon, Rémi. 2010. *Diccionario de la lengua Náhuatl o Mexicana*. Iztapalapa, Mexico: Mújica.

Simons, Ronald, and Charles Hughes. 1985. *The Culture-Bound Syndromes: Folk Illnesses of Psychiatric and Anthropological Interest*. Boston: Kluwer Academic.

Solari, Amara. 2016. "The 'Contagious Stench' of Idolatry: The Rhetoric of Disease and Sacrilegious Acts in Colonial New Spain." *Hispanic American Historical Review* 96, no. 3, 481–515.

Stahle, David W., Edward R. Cook, Malcolm K. Cleaveland, Matthew D. Therrell, David M. Meko, Henri Grissino-Mayer, Emma Watson, and Brian Henry Luckman. 2000. "Tree-Ring Data Document Sixteenth-Century Megadrought over North America." *Transactions American Geophysical Union* 81, no. 12: 121–25.

Sullivan, John, Eduardo de la Cruz Cruz, Abelardo de la Cruz de la Cruz, Delfina de la Cruz de la Cruz, Victoriano de la Cruz Cruz, Sabina Cruz de la Cruz, Ofelia Cruz Morales, Catalina Cruz de la Cruz, and Manuel de la Cruz Cruz. 2016. *Tlahtolxitlauhcayotl: Chicontepec, Veracruz*. Warsaw: IDIEZ/University of Warsaw.

Taggart, James M. 1997. *The Bear and His Sons: Masculinity in Spanish and Mexican Folktales*. Austin: University of Texas Press.

Terraciano, Kevin. 2010. "Three Texts in One: Book Twelve of the Florentine Codex." *Ethnohistory* 57, no. 1: 51–72.

Terraciano, Kevin. 2014. "Narrativas de Tlatelolco sobre la Conquista de Mexico." *Estudios de Cultura Nahuatl*. 47: 211–35.

Weller, Susan C., Roberta D. Baer, Javier Garcia de Alba Garcia, and Ana L. Salcedo Rocha. 2008. "Susto and Nervios: Expressions for Stress and Depression." *Culture, Medicine and Psychiatry* 32, no. 3, September: 406–20.

White, Richard. 1991. *The Middle Ground: Indians, Empires, and Republics in the Great Lakes Region, 1650–1815*. New York: Cambridge University Press.

# Tepahtihquetl pan ce pilaltepetzin / A Village Healer

Sabina Cruz de la Cruz, *Instituto de Docencia e Investigacion Etnologica de Zacatecas*
Translated by Rebecca Dufendach, *Getty Research Institute*

**Abstract.** Sabina Cruz de la Cruz presents an auto-ethnohistory, an account written in her native language of Nahuatl based on her community experiences with illness and curing in the Huasteca region of Veracruz, Mexico. She documents her work with two curanderos to improve her poor health. The article is an invaluable record of contemporary, indigenous healing dialogue and traditions, some of which have similarities with colonial-era practices. It is an example of a collaboration between an ethnohistorian and an indigenous scholar writing her own history, and such collaborations will strengthen the field of ethnohistory.

**Keywords.** Mexico, auto-ethnohistory, Nahuatl, Nahua, health, salud, illness, enfermedad

## Introduction from Translator

In her explanation of Ethnohistory, Pauline T. Strong (2015: 194) laments that indigenous peoples have not often had the privilege to write their own histories and explains that studies in the field will be strongest "when indigenous and non-indigenous scholars are collaborating side by side." The following essay is one such collaboration, centered on the writings of a Nahua scholar and how she analyzes her own health and healing.

It is a Nahuatl-language account written by Sabina Cruz de la Cruz about her experiences of poor health and healing practices with two healers, or *curanderos*. It is unique as an "auto-ethnohistory" because she writes in her native language of Nahuatl about her experiences in a Nahuatl-speaking community. An auto-ethnohistory is defined by the participation

*Ethnohistory* 66:4 (October 2019) DOI 10.1215/00141801-7683258
Copyright 2019 by American Society for Ethnohistory

of an indigenous person in the telling of their own history and experiences in their native language. Cruz was born in Tecomate, Veracruz, Mexico, and she consulted with a *curandera* from Tecomate and a *curandero* from nearby Tiocuayo, Veracruz. Cruz shares methods of healing far from any hospital setting, methods relied on by many people in urban and rural settings. The essay explains what modern health professionals are beginning to accept by acknowledging social determinants of health: that the definitions and cures for illness are always contextual (US Department of Health and Human Services 2010: sec. 1). Cruz's experiences of illness are directly related to her relations with her parents and broader community.

Unlike the other essays in this special issue, which are written largely by outsiders attempting to understand Mesoamerican healing practices, here is a view from a member of the community. Cruz's interpretations of illness are related to her social and cultural context. As a native speaker, she writes in the language in which the ceremonies were performed, so her record of dialogue is invaluable. Despite being discouraged from speaking in Nahuatl when she was young, Cruz continues to produce scholarship in her native language (Valenzuela 2017). Although the essay is based entirely on her work with two healers, Cruz chose to write it in the third person, perhaps following storytelling traditions to make a parable out of her experiences. Her participation in the healing ceremonies along with her membership in the Huasteca Veracruzana community provide a valuable window into healing practices.

Her essay reveals that contemporary Nahua healing practices are best understood through her multi-layered view. As a scholar, woman, and member of her community, Cruz has unrivaled understanding into how modern healers diagnose and treat illness. As the article reveals, her success in her academic pursuits changes her standing in her community. She shows that her duties as a daughter, such as sending money home, influence the position of her parents. Although best understood as a contemporary account of illness and treatment, Cruz's essay does present some remarkable continuities with colonial practices.

The essay explores the methods and materials used in traditional healing, some of which have changed since the colonial period but some of which have not. Some changes since the sixteenth century surely include the use of soda cans. However, even a critic of ethnographic upstreaming must acknowledge that beverages have and will continue to play an important part of Mesoamerican healing ceremonies (see Knowlton and Dzidz Yam, this issue). Some continuities include the manner of divination. For example, both healers initiated their work by reading kernels of corn and practiced the elimination of objects from the human body. The sixteenth-century encyclopedic work on Nahua culture known as the *Florentine Codex* describes a similar procedure where the activities of healers included casting grains of corn and the removal of foreign objects from the body (Sahagún: [1575–79] 1979: vol. 1, bk. 1, fols. 3v, 36v–37). The essay also describes the sweeping with herb bundles for cleansing, blood sacrifice, and the importance of abstaining from bathing, each practice with some similarities to rituals documented during the colonial period (bk. 2, fols. 123v; 121v–123; 124). There is much more evidence for analysis in this important auto-ethnohistory.

Readers interested in additional research should look to Alan R. Sandstrom's book on a modern Nahuatl-speaking community titled *Corn Is Our Blood* (1991), the collection *Mesoamerican Healers* edited by Sandstrom and Huber (2001), a chapter by Elizabeth Hill Boone (2005), and articles by James Dow (1986, 1984). These preliminary observations on Cruz's essay deserve further examination in the future by scholars who will become more accustomed to auto-ethnohistories as indispensable sources for study. Such collaborations, between ethnohistorians and indigenous scholars writing their own histories, will strengthen the field of ethnohistory.

A note on the translation: I have tried to follow the original Nahuatl text as faithfully as possible, however I made certain changes to better communicate the intent of the text according to my conversations with Cruz. Many of these instances are marked with parentheses but others are matters of word choice. In our efforts to translate an auto-ethnohistory, I have not asked Cruz to change her text in any significant way and continue to respect her choice to write in the third person.

## Tepahtihquetl pan ce pilaltepetzin

Ce tepahtihquetl, tlachixquetl tlen pan ce pilaltepetzin oncah nelhuah-cauhquiya, quipiya miac xihuitl. Tlen tototatahhuan inintlaixmatiliz huan tlen huahcapameh itztoyah pan ni tlalli. Tototatahhuan tlahuel tlaneltocah pan ce tepahtihquetl tlen nouhquiya quimati cualli itequiuh huan tlen quichihua itequiuh xitlahuac. Itztoqueh tlen cualli huan xitlahuac quichichuah inintequiuh huan tlen axcanah cualli inintequih, tiquihtozceh queuhquinon pampa cequin macehualmeh itztoqueh tlen quinpalehuiah ica tequitl pampa tecocoliah.

Naman nicmanextia ce tlamanextili tlen ce ichpocatl, nicpohuaz ce tlamantli ica tlen quipanoc ni macehualli tlen pilaltepetzin tlen Chicontepec, tiquihtozceh axtlen quichihua, zan nemi, quichihua itequiuh, ni cihuatl ya momachtihtoc huan cualli yohui ica itequiuh, inemiliz. Nouhquiya ni ichpocatl ohuih panoc para quichihuaz zo itztoz campa itztoc. Quen quiihtoah pan ni tonemiliz nochi ohuih, zan quena tlan ticnequih tielizceh ce acahya pan tonemiliz monequi ticcencuilizceh timomachtiah.

Tiquihtozceh itztoqueh macehualmeh tlen tecocoliah huan quichihuah zo quitemoah ce tepahtihquetl tlen axcualli itequiuh quichihua. Ni ichpocatl quizqui pan ipilaltepeuh huahcauhquiya, ya yahqui pan ce altepetl ica miac mahmauhtli, peuhqui momachtia meuhcatzan ohuihtic, noque momachtiyaya nouhquiya tequitiyaya, tequitiyaya pan calli, campa quinamacah tlacualli zo ceyoc tequitl, queuhquinon quipiyaya ce quentzin tlaxtlahuilli huan axcanah monequiyaya quitlahtlaniz tomin inintatahhuan. Queuhquinon ya tequitiyaya, tomintzin ica mopalehuihtiyohuiyaya huan nouhquiya queuhquinon quemman mociauhcahuayaya pan caltlamachtihcan yohuiyaya campa itztoqueh itatahhuan ica tomin tlen ya. Yolpaqui ya huan itatahhuan pampa moittayayah, nopayoh ininhuanitztoz ce mahtlactli tonatiuh. Nochi yolpactoqueh.

Zan quena tlen tecocolianih axcanah tlamih. Axcanah huelih cualli quiittah tlan ichpocatl huan itatahhuan paquih huan axcanah mocualaniah. Ni ichpocatl quipiya macuilli iicnihuan huan queuhquinon nochimeh tlen quiztoquehya pan ipilaltepeuh, momachtiah huan tequitih, queuhquinon axcanah quitlahtlaniyayah tomin inintatah. Huan queuhquinon ichpocatl tequitiyaya huan momachtiyaya, quemman quitlamih itlamachtiliz motequicuic zampampa axcanah tlen momachtihqui, zan quena quimachilia cualli tequitl huan tlen ya quinequiyaya tlahuel huan quiamati.

Queuhquinon quicencuilihqui tequiti huan tequiti, quinpalehuihtiuh itatahhuan ica ce tlaxtlahuilli. Miac zo axmiac quinmacayaya tomin. Teipan nouhquiya pan pilaltepetzin nopa ichpocatl itatah ayocacah quinequiyayah quipalehuizceh yon axacah quinequiyayah quimacazceh tequitl. Ya quiilliyayah, quenque quinequi tequitiz huan ya quipiya tomin, huan pampa iconehuan nochi itztoqueh huahca huan momachtihtoqueh. Ni tlacatl mocuezoyaya huan motlahtlaniliyaya quenque queuhnopa quiilliah, ya axcanah mopatlatoc, ya quincencuilia quen nochipa itztoc. Huan axcanah motlepanitta. Yolic, yolic zampa peuhqueh quimacah tequitl, zo peuhquiya huanya mopalehuia cequinoqueh. Zan quena nouhquiya quimati quena quicocoliah, moxicoah pampa ya ayoccanah tlaihyohuia tlahuel.

Miac macehualmeh axtlen hueliz zan quiittah tlen pano pan ce pilaltepetzin pampa zan nochi moixmatih, nochi quimatih huan quiittah tlen ceyoc macehualli inemiliz. Teipan nopayoh pehuaya quiillamiquih, zaniloah ica nopa macehualli inemiliz. Meuhcatzan axcanah quiixmatih cualli.

## Tlacotontli

Naman nicnequi nimechpohuiliz ica ce ichpocatl tlen quichihuiltoqueh tlen axcanah cualli huan quitemohqui cualtlalhuiliztli ica inemiliz huanya ce tepahtihquetl tlen ipilaltepeuh.

Achtohui ni cihuatl yahqui huanya ce tepahtihquetl tlen itatah quiixmati huan quineltoca tlen quichihua, yahqui para ma quitlatemoli, tiquihtozceh ce tlen quichihua xitlahuac itequiuh. Ichpocatl ahci tepahtihquetl ichan huan nopa tepahtihquetl pehua monemilia ica tlen quitehuiz: ce pilhuapaltzin quentzin hueyi, cintlancochtli tlapohualli hueliz ce mahtlactli huan nahui zo caxtolli huan eyi. Quitequihuia popochcomitl, copalli huan nopa ichpocatl, ya quihuica ce pilcantelahtzin huan tomin tlen mahtlactli tlen ica quichihuilizceh nopa tlatemoliztli. Ni ichpocatl nouhquiya quena tlaneltoca ica ni tlanextilli huan yeca ya nouhquiya quitemohua queniuhqui cualli itztoz.

Tepahtihquetl pehua motiochihua campa itlaixpan, tlaihitoa huan campa quipiya nopa huapalli huan cintli, nouhquiya tlahtlani queniuhqui itocah ichpocatl, queniuhqui itzonquizca, huan canin nemi pampa queuhquinon tlahtlani ica totiotzin. Nelnelliya motemaca huan quichihua cualli itequiuh nopa tepahtihquetl. Motiochihua, tlatocaxtia campa itztoc ichpocatl, pampa azta ne nemi itonal, quiahhuia pilcintzin pan imah huan quipanoltia iixco popochcomitl tlen quipiya tlicolli huan teipan quiihtzeloa pan nopa huapalli, huan quitlachilia canin huan queniuhqui huetzih pilcintzitzin. Teipan ya quinillihqui tlen quiitta, queniuhqui itztoc. Quimahcahuaz zampa nopa pilcintzitzin nopa pampa quinequi quiittaz tlan nelnelliya neci quen tlen achtohui, huacca quena quiillia nochi, Tepahtihquetl quiihtoa: "nican neci mitzcocoliah, moxicoah cequinoqueh pampa ta axtlen mitzpoloa, ticpiya tequitl, ticpiya ce cualli tequitl, axcanah tiquincahua motatahhuan inincelti, eli tiquinpalehuia ica ce quentzin tlaxtlahuilli, cualli tiitztoc, ahachica tihuallauh tiquinpaxaloa motatahhuan. Huan cequin axquinequih quiittazceh pampa inihhuantin axcanah queuhquinon itztoqueh zo axcanah huallohuih ininconehuan quinhualpaxaloah ahachica. Ni yeca quichihuah tlen axcualli, quinequih ximoquetza quentzin, nouhquiya quinequih xiohuihti."

Quen pehua momachilia ichpocatl. Ya axcanah itztoc pan ipilaltepeuh huanya itatahhuan, ya nemi pan ceyoc altepetl, quipiya miac xihuitl quiahuac. Huacca quemman huahca itztoc ni cihuatl pehua quicocoa itzontecon, pehua axcanah hueli cualli cochi, temiqui fieroh, axmayana, axyolpaqui. Quemman yohui huanya itatahhuan huacca quinyolmelahuah queniuhqui itztoz zo momachilia. Itatah quiillia monequi motlatemoliz huan ma quichihuilican ce tequitl, ma quicotona tepahtihquetl tlen quipano.

Ichpocatl huan itatah zan quicaquih tlen quinillia tepahtihquetl, tlami tequiti ya, huacca quinillia tlen monequi ma mochihua, zo mocotonaz ni tlen axcualli tequititoqueh. Ya quinillia monequi ma mochihua ce tlacotontli. Huan tlen monequi, quiillia: tlaochpantli (chicome tlamantli xihuitl Santa maria, apazoxihuitl, tepecocah, cocah, talachia, pizteh huan chalchocotl), ce veladorah tlen tonantzin, ce tlen San Judas Tadeo, cantelah, ceboh, huinoh, tzopelatl ce macuilli zo chicuace tlen cuecuetzitzin. Huan tlen nochipa monequi quipixtozceh pan calli huan motequihuia: popochcomitl, copalli, motlalia xochimantli, huan cequinoc tlamantli tlen yohui tlaixpan. Mocahuah, quitlaliah tlen tonatiuh mochihuaz ni tlacotontli huan tlen cahuitl. Quemman mochihua ni tequitl tlen tlacotontli quitlalia ce tonatiuh tlen miercoles, Viernes, sabado zo domingo, ni tonatiuh pampa quiillia chicahuac tonatiuh huan axcanah tlen ica quipehualtia tlen chicueyi tonatiuh.

Tepahtihquetl yohui ichan ichpocatl, nopayoh ya monequi nochi eltozza tlen quiillihqui quemman quitlatemolihqui, quemman ahci tepahtihquetl ya monemilia ica tlatehtectli, quihuica miac ixnezcayotl tlen amatl canactzin (china), nopa tlatehtectli quichihua ica miac piltotiotzitzin tlen iixxayac huan itlacayo quipiya, pampa inihhuantin yoltoqueh: quen iteco tlen atl, ehecatl, tonantzin, totatah, tlitl, tlalli huan cequinoqueh. Nochi nopayoh quinmanextia ica amatl huan nouhquiya pampa quemman tequitiya, ya pehua quintocaxtia nochimeh huan queuhquinon quimacah chicahualiztli pan itequiuh.

Nouhquiya quinemiliah atl, tlen campa quitequihuiah: cuaxilotl icuayo, nehpalli, quitehtequi ciltic huan quiamaneloa queuhquinon quicahuah ma elto pampa ni motequihuia quemman nochi tlamiya quichihua itequiuh, ica tlaahatequia tlaixpan huan campa tlitl. Quemmantzin ica mixxamiah. Tepahtihquetl tlahtlaniz tlicolli tlen ica tlapopochhuiz tlaixpan.

## Quen Pehua Tequiti

Ni tepahtihquetl axcanah mociauhcahua, monemiltiaz, pehua motiochihua tlaixpan, quincamahuia totiotzitzin, quintlahtlania manoh pampa ya tequitiz, quichihuaz ni tequitl, quinequi ma quipalehuican, ma quihuanitztocan, axcanah ma quicahuacan icelti, ma cualli quiza itequiuh tlen quichihuaz ica ni inincihuaconeuh, tlapopochhuia cualli.

Teipan quinotza anque ichpocatl tlen quipahtiz pampa quiochpanaz ica tlaochpantli, cantelah huan nouhquiya ica ce tecciztli, nopa quiahcocui tlaixpan pampa quitequihuiz pan mero tlacotontli. Quemman quiochpana pehua camati ica totiotzitzin huan nouhquiya quitequilia achi huinoh nopa tlaochpantli huan quemman nelnelliya quimachilia cihuatl quena quipiya tlen axcualli ya pehua cochmiqui, zotlahuia.

Queuhquinon quemman tlami quiochpana cihuatl, tepahtihquetl zampa pehua motiochihua tlaixpan huan quimaca nopa cantelah cihuatl ma quitlati huan ma quitlalli tlaixpan. Teipan tepahtihquetl zampa motiochihua zampampa naman motlahtlania ica ce piyo tlen ica quiochpanaz zampa ichpocatl. Quinotza ichpocatl, mocehuia pan ce cuaciyah pehua ica quiochpana cihuatl huan queuhquinon zampa pehua camati ica totiotzitzin.

Tepahtihquetl quemman motiochihua quiihtoa: "Tonanan, totatah nican tiitztoqueh moixtenno, nican moconehuan axcanah mitzilcahuah huan naman nican ticnequih timitzilizceh moxochiconeuh ma quicahuacan ya axtlen quichihua, ya zan quinequi cualli itztoz, tequitiz yehyectzin zan ta ticmati itztoqueh tlen cualanih, tecocolianih. Ni moxochiconeuh axtlen quichihua, xicquixtilican nochi tlen quipechia . . . " Quemman tlamiya, ichpocatl quiahhuia piyo tlen ica quiochpanqueh.

Teipan tepahtihquetl quimictia piyo ica ce tiheraz, quicomichoa pan iquechcuayo huan tlen quiza eztli quiihtzeloa pan amatl tlatehtectli tlen quizoa tlalchi tlen tlaixpan. Piyo tlen quimictia quimaca tenanan zo ichpocatl pampa monequi ma quihuihuitla, ma quitetehtequi pampa quimoloniz huan mocualtlaliz. Nouhquiya quemman motehtequi ni piyo axcanah nelmociloa, monequi eliz inacayo achi huehhueyi huan mocualtlalia zan caltoh (campa quihuica xonacatl, alahhuenoh huan chilli chichiltic tlamoltilli).

Noque mocualtlalia piyo. Tepahtihquetl quichihua tlacotontli tlen ichpocatl para ma quiza tlen quipiya. Motlalia nechca tlahcocalli, tlachixtoc ica caltenno. Nopayoh motlahtlalia nochi tlen quitequihuiz: Tlatehtectli tlen totiotzitzin, ni quitlalia chihueyi totiotzitzin ica miac ixnezcayotl amatl, ce cantelah, ce cebo, popochcomitl, tlalli tlen millah, huinoh, tlaochpantli quitecpana, tecciztli tlen ica quipohpohqui quen achtohui xoxohuic, ce tecciztli iuccitoc . . . huan cequinoc amatlatehtectli tlen tiquihtozceh tlen zaniloah, tlen tecocoliah, tlen quinilliz ma mocehuican axtlen ma quichihuacanyoc pampa ichpocatl ya axtlen quichihua.

Tepahtihquetl pehua motiochihua nopayoh, motlahtlania ica totiotzitztin para ni ichpocatl ma quimanahuican, ma axtlen quipano campa nemi, xicmacacan ce cualli ohtli, ce cualli tequitl, ce cualli cochiliztli . . . queuhquinon huan quitequiltiyahqui huinoh nopa amatlatehtectli. Nopa tecciztli tlen xoxohuic quipitzinihqui huan quitecqui tlalchi huan nopayoh nouhquiya quiitta tlen quiza iixxayac. Huan quihtoaya tlan quena mitzcocoliah zo tlan tlahuel mitzcocoliah. Huan tecciztli tlen iuccitoc ya quitlapana huan quitema nouhquiya tlalchi, pan amatlatehtectli huan pan tlalli tlen millah.

Quemman tlamiya tlacamahuia huanya totiotzitzin, pehua quicui nahui amatl tlen totiotzitzin huan ica nopa tlaochpantli huan quitlahcocotona, ome zo eyi hueltah quichihua queuhquinon, huan zampa quicui tlen polihui huan nouhquiya quichihua queuhquinon huan quiahhuia. Huan zampa quicui ceyoc nahui amatlatehtectli nouhquiya quintlahcocotona, ya axtlami motiochihua, quicencuilia quichihua itequiuh.

Tepahtihquetl ya quiihtoz quezqui polatoh tlacualli ica nochi huan quezqui yohui pan tlaixpan huan quezqui tlalchi. "Ma motlali ome polatoh tlacualli ica tlaxcalli huahcapan huan nahui tlalchi." Nouhquiya motlalia tzopelatl chicuace, ome huahcapan huan nahui echcapan, tazah cafen cencah ome huahcapan huan nahui tlalchi, ica pantzin nouhquiya cehcen pan ce tazah.

Nouhquiya tlahtlalia pan tlitl ica inacaztlan, nopayoh tlahtlaliah nouhquiya quitlaliah ce xochimantli, quitlatia ce cantelah, ce polatoh tlacualli ica tlaxcalli, ce tazah cafen huan ce pantzin. Nopayoh nouhquiya motiochihua tepahtihquetl. Queuhquinon eltoz ce tlatoctzin, noque tiquihtozceh tlacuah totiotzitzin. Teipan tepahtihquetl quiihtoz ma motlamaca tlalli. Monequi ma motlali tlacualli, tlaxcalli huan pantzin pan tlalli. Nouhquiya monequi motecaz achi tzopelatl huan cafen. Queuhuinon teipan quemman tlamiya mochihua, quiihtoa: "naman monequi ma titlacuaca zancehco tlan eltocca inmopapa. Xiccuican tlen motlalihqui, tlacualli xicpihuican." Tlen chaneh pehua quipipihuiya tlacualli tlen motlalih tlaixpan pampa axcanah mihmiyac moteca huan monequi yainon mocuaz, quicuih tzopelatl. Monechcahuiah nochi pan ce mezah huan tlacuah.

Tepahtihquetl quemman tlacuah zan quiihtoa: "nochi cualli quizqui ne niccotonquiya tlen axcualli eltoya, quichiuhtoyah, zan monequi ximochiyacan ce nahui tonatiuh. Ni tlacehuiz. Ayoccanah zanilozceh, axtlen quichihuazceh." "Quena nezqui tlen quichiuhtoyah axcualli, quinequih ma mocehui ichpocatl, axcanah ma quipiya tequitl, nochi tlen axcanah quipalehuiz para quizaz."

Ni ce tequitl tlen mochihua tlen ica quipalehuia macehualli ma tlacehui, axtlen ma quipano tlan quimachilia axcualli itztoc, quence quicotona itequiuh tlen quichihuiltoqueh axcualli. Zan quena tlan quichihua ni tequitl monequi quicenculiz xihxihuitl, axcanah ma quicahuilli pampa queuhquinon nouhquiya totiotzitzin quipalehuizceh quence axcanah quinilcahuah. Huan nouhquiya pampa tlen tecocoliah axcanah mociauhcahuah, inihhuantin quicencuiliah quichihuah tlen axcualli. Yeca ni tlacotontli monequi nouhquiya miac tlatlepanittaliztli huan miac tlaneltoquiliztli. Queuhquinon mopalehuiah cequin macehualmeh tlen pilaltepetzitzin.

## Tlaquihquixtiliztli

Nican nimechpohuiliz ceyoc tequitl tlen quichihua ce tepahtihquetl. Ni itocah Tlaquihquixtiliztli pampa quiquixtia miac tlamantli tlen ticpiya pan ce tlacayoliztli tlen macehualli. Ticmachiliz axtiyolpaqui, titlacayohuahcuallo, zan ticochmiqui, motequiuh tlen ticchihua yolic, mitzcocoz motzontecon chicahuac. Axcanah quipannextia quezqui xihuitl quipiya macehualli, nochimeh hueliz quinpanahci.

Ni tepahtihquetl quichihua tlen achtohui ce tlatemoliztli ica macehualli tlen queuhquinon momachilia. Campa quitequihuia cantelah, amatlatehtectli tlen chicueyi zo nahui totiotzitzin iixxayac, ceboh, popochcomitl, iyatl, huinoh, tlalli, tecciztli xoxohuic huan ce iuccitoc, huan tlaochpantli: quihuica chicome tlamantli xihuitl (Santa maria, apazoxihuitl, tepecocah, cocah, talachia, pizteh huan chalchocotl), quiilpia cehcen tlamantli huan eli chicome tlatzquintli.

Quen achtohui tepahtihquetl ya pehua motiochihua pan tlaixpamitl ica tlen tequitl quichihuaz huanya nopa ichpocatl huan ma quipalehuican, ma quihuanitztocan, ya nouhquiya motlahtlania ma cualli quiza itequiuh. Nican quichihua ce tlatemoliztli tlen itlacayo, ¿tlen quipiya pan itlacayo?, xicnexti tlen quipiya, ¿canin eltoc?

Tepahtihquetl achtohui quichihua ce tlatemoliztli pan ce huapalli zancualli ica cintli ce quezqui itlancoch, ce cantelah huan tomin tlen mahtlactli pezoh, nopayoh pehua motlahtlania ica totiotzitzin nouhquiya, quiihtoa ma neci tlen quipechia ni inmoconeuh. Nopayoh motiochihua, quimapixtoc cintlancochtli, quitocaxtia macehualli tlen quipahtia, quemman tlamizza huacca quiitzeloa nopa cintli pan huapalli huan nopayoh quiitta tlen quipiya macehualli pan itlacayo huan zampa quimahcahuaz cintli para zampa quiittaz zo motemachiz tlen quiitta pan macehualli itlacayo.

Ica ome hueltah quena quiillizza ichpocatl huanya itatahhuan tlen quiittac. Quiihtoa: "Quena, quena tlapihpiya ne ya, huan quipiya miac tlamantli tlen axcualli." Tepahtihquetl iuhcatzan quiitta tlen quipiya ya axcanah teyolmelahua nelneliya tlen quiitta, axcanah quiihtoa pampa hueliz motemahmatia ichpocatl zo nouhquiya inintatahhuan. Zan quena quinillia tlen monequi quihuicazeh para moquixtiliz tlen quipiya ichpocatl. Quitlalliah tonatiuh quemman yazeh zampa ica nochi tlamantli tlen monequi, para ica tequitiz huan quiquixtiz pan itlacayo ichpocatl tlen quipiya. Monequi iyatl, huinoh, ahoh nochi ni tlamantli achi mihmiyac.

Yohuih ininchan monemiliah ica tlamantli tlen monequi para quitlaquihquixtilizceh ichpocatl, pan ni yahualli tiquihtozceh ni ichpocatl huan itatahhuan axhuelih cochih, zan quimahttoqueh, quinehnehuiliah tlen quipiyaz ininconeuh.

Toniliz zo huiptlatiliz yohuih zampa ichan tepahtihquetl ica nochi tlamantli tlen monequi, zampa tepahtihquetl quicui tlen quihuicah, quicualtlalia quen monequi, quemman eltocca pehua motiochihua, quincamahuia totiotzitzin, pampa ya tequitiz. Ichpocatl motlaquixtilia huan mocehuia

pan ce cuaciyah. Tepahtihquetl quiochpanaz ica tlaochpantli huan cantelah. Motiochihtiuh axcanah moquetza. Teipan quitlatia cantelah tlaixpan.
Ichpocatl mocehuiz pan ce cuaciyah, huan ya pehua motiochihua, tlai-
hihtohti nochi ica macehualli tlen quipahtia, nican pehuaya quiochpana
para quitlaquihquixtiliz ica nopa tlachihchihualli pahtli (huinoh, ahoh,
xihuitl Santa Maria, Iyatl). Yainon quicualtlalia pan ce tecomitl zan tlen
zancualli.

Quitoxomiltiuh pan itlacayo cihuatl pehua pan itzontecon, yahtiuh
icampan, pan iahcol, iyolihcan, ielchititlan, pan iihti, pan imetz, pan itlan-
cuah, pan iicxi huan quitlaltiuh tecomitl campa quitzacuiltiuh tlen quiza
pan itlacayo, queuhquinon tlami quiochpana. Cihuatl motlaquentia, zan
quena ya momachilia xoxocoxtoc, zotlahuia axcanah nelhueli motlaquentia
icelti, huan nouhquiya monequi quipalehuizeh pampa cuaixpoyahui huan
cececui, monequi nelcualli mopiquiz pampa quiochpanqueh ica huinoh
huan axcanah cualli tlan quiahciz ehecatl, hueliz mococoz maz. Yeca monequi momocuitlahuiz.

Tepahtihquetl quiihtoa: "Eltocca, nitlanquiya, nican eltoc tlen quizqui
tlan inquinequih inquiittazceh. Zan ya quena axcanah cualli ma quiitta zo
tlan momachilia cualli, quipiya huerzah, nican eltoc." Huanquinon quiittah zan itatahhuan huan axcanah quiilihqueh ininconeuh huacza tlen
quizqui. Teipan tepahtihquetl quiinillia tlen ma quichihuacan quemman
ahcizceh pan ininchan. Tepahtihquetl: "Nopa cantelah tlen motlati achtohui monequi motlatiz ce quentzin quemman inahcizceh huan queuhquinon motlatiz nahui tonatiuh mohmoztlah huan nouhquiya ni inmoci-
huapil axcanah monequi maltiz nahui tonatiuh, axcanah ma panquiza,
axcanah ma tenamiqui, zan calihtic ma itzto. Nouhquiya axcanah xiquillican
namantzin tlen quizqui pan itlacayo, pampa motemahmatiz." Queuhquinon
mochihua pampa queuhquinon cualli quizaz tequitl tlen ticchiuhqueh.

Quemman ahcih ininchan quichihuah tlen quinillihqui tepahtihquetl
huan ichpocatl moteca campa cochi huan cualli mopiqui. Queuhquinon
cualli cochi huan ihza tonilia, ica yahuatzinco huan nocca yahyamaniya
nochi itlacayo. Axtlen quichihua zan queuhquinon yolic quipanotiz ayoc-
tlen quimachiliz. Nouhquiya quimachiliz itlacayo acazotic pampa tlen qui-
pixtoya quence quipechtoya huan yainon quichihuayaya ma zan zotlahuia,
ma cochmiqui, ma axmayana. Pano tonatiuh huan ahci tlen nahui tonatiuh,
ni ichpocatl maltia ica ce xihuitl tlen itocah tamalxihuitl, mocualtlalia ni
xihuitl zan ica atl. Achtohui ni xihuitl motzatzayatza ciltic huan teipan
moaquechia pan ce cobetah hueyi, nopayoh monequi eltoz quentzin huah-
cahuaz zo tlan mocualtlalia ica yahuatzinco hueliz ica tlahcotona zo tiotlac
huelizza maltia ichpocatl, cualli motehtequilia pan nochi itlacayo huan pan
itzontecon.

Nouhquiya teipan quemman maltiyaya huacca quena quilliah tlen quizqui pan itlacayo:

- Tomin: Ni tomin eliyaya huehhueyi huan quence huahcapatomin, nouhquiya quipiyaya hueliz miac xihuitl eltoya pan itlacayo, neciyaya yayahuic.
- Cantelah: Eltoya ome cantelahcotoctli nezqui quence yancuic nocca hueliz yancuic quichihuiltoqueh tequitl tlen axcualli huan yeca queuhquinon nezqui.
- Omitl: Ome omitl cuecuetzitzin nouhquiya hueliz ayicanah tlahuel huahcahua neciyaya nocca chipahuac.
- Amatlatehtectli: Ni amatl quizqui hazta yayahuic hueliz huahcauhquiya eltoc pan itlacayo.
- Tetl: Quizqui ome tetl zan tlen zancualli hueyi, yayahuic huan yehyectzin petlanih huan alaxtique.

Nochi ni tlamantli tlen quizqui pan ichpocatl itlacayo tlan axquemman tiquitta zo axticcactoc temahmati, huan nouhquiya ica ni tequitl monequi timomocuitlahuiz tlahuel, nouhquiya axcanah hueliz tiyaz mocelti para timochihuiliz ni tequitl, monequi ma mitzmocuitlahuican.

Ichpocatl quiihtoa: "Quena nimotemahmatihqui tlahuel pampa axquemman niquitztoya zo nechchihuiltoyah queuhquinon, nimochoquilihqui nouhquiya, huan nimotlahtlaniyaya quenque zo queniuhqui itztoqueh tlen techcocoliah tlahuel, ce zo ome yahualli na axcualli nicochqui, pampa zanya nicmahttoya, tlen nechquixltihqueh pan notlacayo." Itatahhuan quiyolchicauhqueh, quiilliyayah axcanah ximocuezo, axcanah xichoca, monequi timoyolchicahuiliz huan ticcencuiliz moohuiuh, ica motequiuh, queuhquinon miac tlamantli tlen cualli quiilliyayah ininconeuh.

Ica ni tlamantli nouhquiya timotlahtlaniz quenque zo queniuhqui ni tlamantli tlen quizqui eltoya pan itlacayo macehualli huan axcanah neci, miac quiihtoah zan totiotzin quiitta huan quimati quenque pano ni tlamantli huan nouhquiya zan quimatih tlen tecocoliah, tlen moxicoah. Pan ni tlaltepactli tiehelihuih tiitztoqueh.

Ni ome tequitl huahcauhquiya mochihua, quichiuhtihualtoqueh tlen tototatahhuan huan tlen maz huahcauhquiya tetahtzitzin, inihhuantin tlahuel mopahtiyayah huan inihhuantin quinnextiltehtoqueh tlen naman totatahhuan huan naman tohhuantin technextiliah pampa tecocolianih nochipa itztoqueh, axcanah tlamih. Ica ni tlacotontli huan tlaquihquixtiliztli ce momocuitlahuia ica miac tlamantli achtohui quena, tlen mitzcocoliah nouhquiya ica ce cocoliztli tlen mitzpano pan motlacayo, ce ehecatl, tlan titzonteconcuahcuallo. Tlan ticnequi ma cualli tiyaz pan moohuiuh, motequiuh, nochi campa tinemi axtlen ma mitzpano.

Zan monequi nelnelliya tictlaliz zo ticchihuaz ica moyollo pampa queuhquinon quena cualli quizaz tlen ta ticnequi ticchihuaz huan cualli tiitztoz, ticchihuaz tlen quiihtoz tepahtihquetl. Ni tequitl hueliz mocecuilia teipan axcanah quemman polihuiz pampa quena zampa quinnextiltiyohuih tlen mozcaltihtiyohuih

# A Village Healer

A healer, a powerful person in a village, has existed for a long time, for many years. Our grandparent's knowledge, the knowledge of our ancestors, is in this land. Our grandparents truly trusted in the healer, in a healer who knows how to do good or straight work. There are those good ones who make their work straight and those who do not do good work. We say this because some indigenous people, or *macehualmeh*, perpetuate bad works because they have hate.

Now I will show an example of a young woman, I will tell about a thing that happened to this indigenous person, *macehualli*, from the village of Chicontepec. We say that she has not done anything (bad), she only lives (in peace), does her work. This woman has studied and does well in her work and life. It was difficult for this woman to be where she is (it was not easy). As they say, in our lives everything is difficult, only if we want to be somebody in life is it necessary to study.

We say that there are people who have hate and find a healer who does bad works. The young woman left her village a long time ago. She went to the city with much fear, and she began to study although it was difficult. While she studied she also worked in a house where they sold food or worked in other little jobs. Therefore, she had a little money, so it was not necessary to ask her parents for money. In this way, she worked and helped with the money. When she had breaks from school she went to visit her parents with her own money. She made herself and her parents happy because she went and was with them for ten days. Everyone was happy.

It was only that those who had hate did not stop. They could not stand to see the young woman and her parents happy and that they did not fight (amongst themselves). The woman had five brothers and sisters and all of them had left the village. They studied, worked, and did not ask for money from their parents. The woman worked and studied, and when she finished her studies she found work. The work was not in the field she studied, but she felt good about the work, she wanted it and liked it.

In this way she worked while helping her parents, sometimes she gave them a lot and sometimes she gave them a little money. Though afterwards, no one in the village wanted to give the father of the woman any work. They said, why do you want to work when you already have money, and because all your children are living far away and have studied. The man was saddened and asked why they would say such things. He had not changed; he had stayed the same. He was not arrogant. Little by little, they began to give him work and he began to help them again. Only in this way did he know that they had hate, that they envied him because he did not suffer as much as they did.

Many people cannot stand to see the good life of another person. It is because they do not have it (such a good life) and because everyone knows each other (in the village). Much later, people began to watch and talk about a person's life even though they do not know them well.

## The Cutting of the Bad

Now I want to tell about a woman to whom they had done things that were not good, and she looked for the cure for her life with the healer of her village.

First, this woman went to see a healer known to her father and he believed in what the healer did. The healer was one who did correct or straight work. She went for the healer to perform a search (on her). When the young woman arrived at the house of the healer, he began to prepare all that he was going to use: a large board and fourteen or eighteen kernels of corn. He utilized the incense burner, the incense copal. The young woman brought a candle and a ten-piece coin. All of which they would use to perform the search (on her). The young woman also believes in the custom and because of this belief she was in search of well-being.

The healer began to pray at the altar, he prayed where they had the board and the corn (below the altar). He asked the name of the young woman, her last name and where she lived, because in this way he could implore the gods. The truth is that the healer always did good work. He prayed and identified the home (outside the village) of the young woman because that is where her soul walked. He blew on the corn in his hand and passed it above the incense burner of copal and then threw the corn on the board and read how the kernels fell. The healer told them what he saw, how it was. He threw the corn kernels again because he wanted to see if it was true what he saw first, then he told her everything. The healer said, "Here I see that they hate you, some have jealousy because you lack for nothing, you have work, you have good work, you do not abandon your parents, you always help them with a little money, it is good, you regularly visit your parents. There are some who do not want to see you (happy) because they do not have what you have, or their children do not visit so reliably. Because of this they do bad, they want to slow you down, they also want you to struggle."

The young woman felt bad symptoms. She was not in the village with her parents. She had lived for many years outside the village. Therefore, when she was outside the village, she began to feel headaches, she began to sleep poorly, had ugly dreams, she didn't feel hunger, she was not happy. When she went to be with her parents, she informed them how she was or how she was feeling. Her father told her that she needed to have a search and a ritual work performed, that the healer would cut or break what was happening (to the woman).

The young woman and her father only listened to what the healer said, when he finished working, then he told them what was needed in order to cut the bad that had been done. He told them it was necessary to perform a ceremony of cutting called *tlacotontli*. He told them that the following items were needed: a bunch of herbs (for the sweeping) (seven types of herbs, leaf of Saint Mary, a type of herb similar to ezpazote, small anona fruits, anona fruit, *talachia*, capulin, and guayaba), a candle of la Virgen and one of Saint Judas Tadeo, a candle, a candle made of fat called *cebo*, alcohol, and five or six small cans of soda. The things the healer always needed and always had at home to use were: the incense burner, the incense copal, various vases, some for the altar. They agreed on a day and the hour to perform the cutting ceremony called *tlacotontli*. The ceremony is on Wednesdays, Fridays, Saturdays, or Sundays because they are strong days and they are not the first days of the week.

The healer went to the house of the woman. There, they already had all the necessary items from when they performed the search. When the healer arrived, he prepared the paper cuttings. He had many colors of tissue paper (*papel de China*). With the paper cuttings he made many gods, their faces and bodies. They are alive: like the god of water, wind, of la Virgen, of our father Jesus Christ, fire, the earth, and others. All of these can appear in the paper cuttings and because he (the healer) was already working, he began to name all of them. In this way he gave force to the work.

Then they prepared the water. They used the banana plant, the nopal, and pitaya. They cut them into small pieces and they stirred with water. Then they left it because it would be used when they were done with the work. They put the water on the altar close to the fire. Sometimes they washed their faces. These three items, the banana plant, the nopal, and the pitaya, are used because they are foamy and cold. They indicate calm and they make it slippery when there are problems. The healer asked for the coals with which he would pass copal smoke (at the altar).

## How the Work Began

The healer did not rest, he continued preparing. He began to pray at the altar, he spoke with the gods, he asked for permission because he was going to work. He needed them to help him, to be with him, to not leave him alone, for his work with their daughter to come out well. He passed the copal smoke.

Afterward he called to the woman, the woman who he would cure. He was going to perform a cleansing with the bunch of herbs, the candle, and the egg. These he had kept on the altar because he would use them during the ceremony of the cutting of the bad called *tlacotontli*. When the cleansing began, he spoke with the gods and he poured a bit of the alcohol over the bunches of herbs. When the woman truly felt that she had something bad, she began to feel sleepy, she felt weak.

The healer finished the cleansing of the woman in this way. He prayed at the altar and he gave the candle to the woman so that she would light it and put it on the altar. Afterward the healer prayed with the chicken, with it he would perform another cleansing on the woman. He called to the woman that she would sit in a chair and he began to perform the cleansing. Again, he began to communicate with the gods.

As he prayed the healer said, "Our mother, our father, here we are in front of you, here your children do not forget you. Now we want that your daughter asks you that she should be left alone. Nothing (bad) should be done to her, she only wants to be healthy and work well. It is only that you know that there are those who become angry, those who have hate. This, your daughter, has not done anything, she only wants to be well. Remove from her everything that weighs her down . . . " When he was done, he breathed on the chicken, the same chicken with which he had completed the cleansing.

Afterward the healer killed the chicken with scissors. He pierced the neck and with the blood he bathed the paper cuttings that he kept at the foot of the altar. Then he gave the dead chicken to the mother or the daughter because they would need to pluck the feathers and cut it, boil it, and prepare it. When they cut the chicken, they did not make small pieces, they would need bigger pieces of meat to prepare in broth (of onions, mint, and crushed red chile).

While they prepared the chicken, the healer continued with the ceremony of the cutting of the bad called *tlacotontli* with the woman to find out what ailed her. He positioned himself in the middle of the house, looking toward the outside. There he put all that he would use: the paper cuttings of the gods, eight gods of many colors, the candle, the candle of fat, the copal incense burner, some earth or dirt from the cornfield, alcohol, the bunches of the herbs, the raw egg used to complete the first cleansing, a cooked egg, and other paper cuttings referring to those that talk and those that have hate. Those that will say what they feel but are unable to do anything because the woman had done nothing wrong.

The healer began to pray there (at the place of the offerings), in his prayers he asked the gods that they protect the woman. He prayed that nothing would happen where she walked, that they bring a good path, good work, and good sleep. He splattered the alcohol on the cuttings. He broke the raw egg onto the ground and there appeared the face of the bad. He said that "Yes they hate you and it is a lot of hate they feel for you." Then he broke the cooked egg onto the ground, onto the cuttings and the dirt from the cornfield.

When he finished praying to the gods, he began to take four of the cuttings and broke the bunches of herbs at the middle. Two or three times he did in this way, and he blew on them. Again he took the other four cuttings and broke them, he did not finish praying, he continued with his work.

The healer would decide on the number of plates, how many went to the altar and how many went to the earth. He said, "Put two plates of food with tortillas above and four below." He also put six sodas, two above and four below, and cups of coffee the same, two above and four below, accompanied with bread.

They also placed offerings on the side of the fire. There they put the offering of a vase, they lit a candle, and also placed a plate of food with tortilla, a cup of coffee with bread. The healer prayed there as well. There the offerings stayed for a while; we say that the gods eat. Afterward the healer would say give food to the earth. It was necessary to put tortillas and bread on the earth. It was also necessary to pour out a bit of the soda and the coffee. When he was done doing this, he said: "Now it is necessary that we eat together if the tortillas are ready. Take what was given as offering, the food, and add a little more." The female head of the household began to add more food. She put it on the altar because she had not served a lot and they would need to eat. She took the soda. Everyone came to the table and ate.

The healer, as he ate, said, "Everything came out well during the cutting of the bad ceremony that we have done, it is now only necessary that we wait four days. It will calm down. Do not speak, do not do anything. I saw well that they (those with hate) had done bad, they want to slow down the woman, to make it so she does not have work. All the things that will not help her come out on top."

They (the healers) do this work to help calm the people, that nothing happens to them. But if one does this work, it is necessary to continue it every year. Do not leave it because the gods will help you, they will not forget you. Also, the hate does not rest, they (those with hate) will continue to do bad. Because of this the ceremony of cutting the bad called *tlacotontli* deserves much respect and much faith. In this way it helps some people in the villages.

## Cleansing

Here I will explain another type of work that a healer performs. It is called a cleansing because it takes many things out of the body of a person. You will feel as though you are not happy, you will have body aches, fatigue, you do your work slowly, and you have headaches. It does not matter the age of the person. This could happen to anyone.

The woman healer first completed a search with the person who felt this way. In it, she used a candle, paper cuttings with four or eight faces of the gods, a white candle, a copal incense burner, a cigarette, alcohol, dirt, one raw and one cooked egg, and bunches of herbs. The bunches of herbs contained seven different types of herbs: seven types of herbs, leaf of Saint Mary, a type of herb similiar ezpazote, small anona fruits, anona fruit, *talachia*, capulin, and guayaba. The healer tied up each type of herb making seven bundles.

First, the healer began to pray at the altar. She prayed on the type of work to be done with the woman, that they (the gods) help her, that they accompany her. The healer also asked that the work turn out well. Here she made the search of the body, asking "What did she have in her body? Show what you have. Where is it?"

The healer made a search on a medium board with corn, a few kernels, a candle, and a coin piece of ten pesos. She began to ask the gods to see what worried the woman. She prayed, she had in her hand the kernels of corn, she named the person she was going to cure, when she finished, she dropped the kernels on the board. There she saw what the person had in her body. She threw the kernels once again to confirm what she saw in the body of the person.

At the second turn the healer told the woman and her parents what she saw. She said "Yes, yes, this woman has something, and she has many things that are not good." Although the healer saw what the woman had, she did not tell the truth of what she saw. The healer did not say it because it could frighten the woman and her parents. She only told them it was necessary to take out what the woman had (in her body). They agreed on a day when they would go again with all the necessary items. They would go to work and take out the things in the woman's body. They needed these things in good portions: a cigarette, alcohol, and garlic.

The woman and her parents prepared all the necessary things to rid the woman of the affliction. During that night the woman and her parents did not sleep well. They were thinking and analyzing their daughter's affliction. The following day, or the third day, they went again to the house of the healer with all of the necessary items. The healer took what they brought and prepared them as needed. When she was ready she began to pray. She spoke with the gods because she was going to work. The woman removed all her clothing and sat in a chair. The healer swept her with the bunches of herbs and the candle. The healer continued to pray and did not stop praying. Then she lit the candle on the altar.

The woman sat in the seat and the healer began to pray. She spoke to the person she was going to cure. She swept in order to remove the afflictions with the medicinal remedies (alcohol, garlic, leaf of Saint Mary, cigarette). These she prepared in a medium gourd cup. She went scrubbing the body of the woman (with the prepared medicine). She began with her head, then the cheeks, the shoulders, the chest, the ribs, the stomach, the legs, the knees, and the feet. She would put into the container the extra (of the prepared medicine) that fell off the body. In this way she finished sweeping her. The woman dressed, she felt weak and nauseous. She could not dress herself well alone. She needed help because she felt sick and was cold. She needed to cover herself well because they had swept her with alcohol. It was not good to be in the blowing wind because the woman could become sicker. Due to this they needed to be careful. The healer said, "Now it is done, I am done, here is what came out, if you would like to see. If she is not well enough, she should not look, but if she feels well, here it is." Then her parents saw but they did not tell their daughter immediately what had come out.

Afterward, the healer told them what to do once they arrived at the house. The healer said, "Light this candle, the one the woman had lit first, when you arrive at the house, and light it for four consecutive days. Do not bathe your daughter for four days. She cannot go out and she should not receive visitors, she should only be inside. Also do not tell her now what came out because she will become frightened." They did this because they wanted the work to come out well.

When they arrived at home, they did what the healer had asked. The woman lay down in her room and covered herself well. She slept well and woke up the next morning and she still felt without energy throughout her body. She did not do anything. Little by little she passed the days without feeling anything. She felt her body was light and crushed. Because of this she felt weak, sleepy, and without hunger. The four days passed, and the woman bathed in a bath of water made with the leaf called the leaf of the tamale. First, they broke the leaf up into small pieces and then soaked them in a large bucket for a good while. If it was prepared in the morning or perhaps by midday or afternoon, the woman would be able to bathe. She poured it over her whole body and head.

After bathing then they told her what came out of her body:

- Pieces of money: the money pieces were large, and they seemed to be from an older time. It also seemed like they had been in her body a long time because they were black.
- Candle: there were pieces of candle that seemed newer. The pieces must have been from bad works done recently.
- Bones: two small bones that also appeared newer because they were still white.
- Paper cuttings: the paper cuttings were black so perhaps they had been in her body a long time.
- Rocks: two rocks came out that were fairly large. They were black, pretty, shiny, and smooth.

All of these things came out of the woman's body. If you have never seen it or heard of it (the things that come out of the body), it can scare you. During this kind of work, it is also necessary that you take care, you cannot go alone, you need someone to take care of you.

The woman explained, "Yes, I was very scared because I had never seen nor had anything done like this, I also cried. I asked myself why and how it was that they hated me so much. One or two nights I could not sleep. I could only think of what had been taken out of my body." Her parents gave her strength and told her not to be sad. They told her not to cry, to be strong and continue on her path, with her work, they said many things like this to their daughter.

About this ceremony you may ask how is it that these things came out of the body that a person cannot see? Many say that only god sees and knows why these things happen. Only god knows those who have hate, those who have envy. In this world we are different.

These two ceremonies were performed a long time ago. Our grandparents and the oldest people performed the ceremonies and they taught them to our parents today. Now they teach them to us because there are always those who have hate, they do not stop. With the cutting and the cleansing of the body ceremonies one can protect oneself from many things. First, the hate is a disease that passes into your body, like an air, like a very strong headache. If you want to do well in your path, in your work, every-where you live, nothing bad will happen.

The truth is that one must do it (the ceremonies) with your heart and in this way, things turn out well. If you do what the healer says you will be well and the things you want to do will be good. This type of work will always continue. It (knowledge of the ceremonies) will not be lost because they will teach it again and it will grow.

It is necessary that we do not forget this custom, that we do it every year. Perhaps when the new year begins, at the end of the year, or when one can. It is necessary that we do not forget this type of work. In this way the gods will not forgets us, we have them present and they have us.

## References

Boone, Elizabeth Hill. 2005. "In Tlamatinime: The Wise Men and Women of Aztec Mexico." In *Painted Books and Indigenous Knowledge in Mesoamerica*, Pub. 69, edited by Elizabeth Hill Boone, 9–25. New Orleans: Middle American Research Institute, Tulane University.

Dow, James. 1984. "Symbols, Soul, and Magical Healing among the Otomí Indi-ans." *Journal of Latin American Lore* 10, no. 1: 3–21.

Dow, James. 1986. "Universal Aspects of Symbolic Healing: A Theoretical Synthesis." *American Anthropologist* 88, no. 1: 56–69.

Huber, Brad R., and Alan R. Sandstrom. 2001. *Mesoamerican Healers*. Austin: University of Texas Press.

Polanco, Edward Anthony. 2018 "'I Am Just a *Tiçitl*': Decolonizing Central Mex-ican Nahua Female Healers, 1535–1635." *Ethnohistory* 65, no. 3: 441–63.

Sahagún, Bernardino de. (1575–79) 1979. *El Códice Florentino de Bernardino de Sahagún*. 3 vols. Mexico City: Secretaría de Gobernación.

Sandstrom, Alan R. 1991. *Corn Is Our Blood: Culture and Ethnic Identity in a Contemporary Aztec Indian Village*. Norman: University of Oklahoma Press.

Strong, Pauline T. 2015. "Ethnohistory." In vol. 8 of *International Encyclopedia of the Social and Behavioral Sciences*, 2nd ed., edited by James D. Wright, 192–97. New York: Elsevier.

US Department of Health and Human Services. 2010. *Healthy People 2020: An Opportunity to Address the Societal Determinants of Health in the United States*. Secretary's Advisory Committee on National Health Promotion and Disease Prevention Objectives for 2020, July 26.

Valenzuela, Liliana. 2017. "As Nahuatl Wanes in Mexico, UT Instructor Tries to Keep Language Alive." *Austin American-Statesman*, June 15. www.statesman .com/news/20170615/as-nahuatl-wanes-in-mexico-ut-instructor-tries-to-keep -language-alive.

# Ossified and Materialized Selves in Three Manuscripts of Colonial Guatemala: Connections with the Sacred Instrumentality of Bone

Servando Z. Hinojosa, *University of Texas Rio Grande Valley*

**Abstract.** Guatemalan colonial-period documents have proven valuable for revealing Maya thinking about bone, especially how Mayas imbued bones with personal identity. At key moments in the narratives of three Guatemalan manuscripts, the *Rabinal Achi, Xpantzay Cartulary,* and *Pop Wuj,* Mayas materialized the self of important individuals through their bones, treating the bones at times like captives. By doing this, colonial-era Mayas were revealing their ideational linkages with Mayas from the Classic and Postclassic periods who practiced ancestor veneration using bones. In this network of practices, Classic-, Postclassic-, and colonial-era Mayas linked human bones to enduring personal forces and used bones to support claims of ancestry to specific people. This study explores this feature of Maya life, and then analyzes how Mayas of the last hundred years now value bone more for other, non-ancestral ritual utilities. They have shifted from treating certain bones as a materialization of self to viewing bones in terms of the practical potentialities the bones encase, employing a mode of engagement exemplified by Tz'utujiil Maya bonesetters who treat broken bones with sacralized bones and bone surrogates. This work examines how bone use has oscillated between these two modes, contrasting how Mayas of the Classic, Postclassic, and colonial periods treated certain bones as a materialization of self against how Mayas of more recent decades have come to emphasize the sacred instrumentality of bone and put it to active use.

**Keywords.** Guatemala, colonial manuscript, Maya, bone, ossified self

## Introduction

When Maya scholar Luis Enrique Sam Colop (2012: 53–54) translated the word *baq* as "bone" and "skull" in his edition of the *Popol Wuj,* his

*Ethnohistory* 66:4 (October 2019)  DOI 10.1215/00141801-7683276
Copyright 2019 by American Society for Ethnohistory

translation of this word describing Hun Hunahpu's head in the calabash tree was consistent with that of earlier scholars. Numerous translators of this highland Maya document have attributed one or both of these meanings to this word, alternatively spelled *bac* or *bak* (de León Valdés and López Perén 1985; Recinos, Goetz, and Morley 1972; Tedlock 1985; Villacorta C. and Rodas N. 1927). Sam Colop's gloss of *baq* as "bone" is also consistent with the primary meaning of *baq* and its cognates in many Maya languages (Burdick 2010: 124). But it is by considering *baq* in a larger sense, as "captive," that we can better appreciate how colonial-, Postclassic-, and likely, Classic-era Mayas considered excarnate bone not merely a body part but an ideal material in which to encase a person's identity. Of particular interest here is how, during the colonial period, Mayas firmly anchored the identities of individuals in bone in episodes contained not just in the K'iche' *Pop Wuj* but in other Maya manuscripts, including the K'iche' *Rabinal Achi* and the Kaqchikel *Xpantzay Cartulary*. Documents like these have proven especially valuable in revealing Maya thinking about bone, particularly how Mayas have long imbued bones with personal identity. At key narrative moments in these three colonial manuscripts, Mayas materialized the self of important individuals through their bones, treating the bones like the persons themselves. By doing this, colonial-era Mayas were not only writing about ossified selves, they were showing their ideational linkages with their Postclassic- and Classic-period forerunners who practiced ancestor veneration using bones and who used bones as trophies (Burdick 2010: 120–21; Scherer 2015: 20). In the process, colonial-era Mayas were also revealing how human bone could contain special instrumental powers, ones that would eventually increase in prominence and even eclipse preconquest Maya ideas that linked bones to ancestors.

By examining the narrative treatment of human bone in three documents of colonial Guatemala, this study explores how colonial-era (1524–1821 CE) Mayas valued bone for the imprinting of personal identities, and situates this thinking within a framework of ideas centered on ancestry extending back to the times of their Postclassic- (900–1524 CE) and Classic-period (200–900 CE) forebears. It then analyzes how Maya groups of the twentieth and twenty-first centuries, with an emphasis on those in Guatemala, have come to value bone more for other, non-ancestral ritual utilities. Mayas have shifted from treating certain bones as a materialization of self to viewing bones largely in terms of the practical potentialities they encase. Mayas now emphasize a broader sacred instrumentality of bones, employing a mode of engagement exemplified, I argue, by Tz'utujiil Maya bonesetters today who treat broken bones with bones and bone surrogates. The diagnostic and treatment work of these Guatemalan Maya bonesetters reveals a sacralized regard for bone that does not impute an ancestral character on bones themselves. For the bonesetters, while bones and bone surrogates do contain sacred qualities, these qualities matter only in the context of healing, when they apply them to instrumental effect. In this way their approach to bone aligns with a larger shift in Maya thinking about bone, one prioritizing an instrumental view over an ancestral view of this material. Taking the colonial data and this ethnographic data into account, then, I examine how bone use has oscillated between these two modes, contrasting how Mayas from the colonial and preceding eras treated certain bones as ossified selves against how Mayas of the last several decades have come to emphasize the sacred instrumentality of bone and put it to active use.

Important considerations should be raised here, though, about the degree to which the cultural features of Maya groups, separated by centuries, can be compared. James Axtell (1979: 3) has pointed out that to "gauge the degree of change that occurs in cultures" it is useful to examine a single cultural group across a vast sweep of time. This allows us to keep the focus on what can vary within that group. But while time depth affords a way to examine how a group changes, this article is not claiming that Mayas on one end of the diachronic scale (i.e., Classic period) are culturally equivalent to Mayas on the other end of the scale (i.e., modern era) and that their ideational systems are identical. Still, because past and present-day Mayas have been clearly shown to be related in terms of languages, cosmology, diet, and technology, tentative comparison is viable between them. That these Mayas moreover occupy a "contiguous ethnographic province," to use a term favored by William N. Fenton (1962: 13) when describing a condition cultural groups should have to better track changes in them, makes cultural features of past and present Mayas suitable for cautious comparison. This is all the more true since the evidence shows not that Maya ideas about bone have remained frozen in time, but that they have in fact changed. And as Mayas and their priorities have continued changing, they have continued shaping their present using human bone and its analogues in line with their needs.

## Materializing Self in the Colonial Period

During the colonial period, Mayas wrote and dictated narratives that revealed a great interest in materializing self in bone, especially when it came to foregrounding ancestrality and establishing a person's ties to an illustrious forebear. By "materializing self" I here refer to the making of conscious efforts to anchor the identities of select deceased persons in material objects and to bring the qualities of those past persons into a living present. It also refers to the overall outcome of these efforts to localize these past persons in material objects. This typically includes making the affected objects available for manipulation to bring about certain outcomes in a social context. Strong evidence for the deliberate materialization of self among Postclassic and Classic Mayas lies in the pages of colonial-era Maya texts like the *Rabinal Achi*, the *Xpantzay Cartulary*, and the *Pop Wuj*, works put to paper after the conquest but stemming from preconquest Maya experience. In each of these documents we see bones used as concentrations of self, and more important, the role that these bones played in furthering the agency of individuals that beheld or wielded these objects.

Turning first to the *Rabinal Achi*, a dramaturgical work written in K'iche' whose earliest written iterations extend to the sixteenth century (Tedlock 2003: 2), we note an important episode in which bones seemingly materialize a protagonist. In this document, certain human bones are described as being carved, set in metal, and kept by the ruler named Hobtoh, actions done primarily to highlight the identity of the person whose body the bones came from. In the text, a central character, Cawek, holds a calabash drinking cup before those who will soon execute him and rhetorically asks whether he is beholding the cranium of his grandfather or his father. He then wonders aloud whether the same will be done with his own skull, whether his own skull and face will be reconstructed with paint (Cardoza y Aragón 1972: 73–74). Were this to be so, Cawek exclaims, his descendants and vassals would evermore recognize his skull and honor him. He refers to his arm bone as a rod mounted in precious metal that will create a tumult in the fortress, and to his leg bone as the beater of the great and small drum, causing trembling in Heaven and Earth (74). The material preservation of Cawek's bones ensures that his glory, and that of his house, will be secured. That the performed *Rabinal Achi* drama bears little likeness to colonial Spanish dances (Tedlock 2003: 11–14) is significant because this suggests that the text precedes the colonial period in both form and ideational content.

Cawek recognizes a person's immortality in ossified form in a manner similar to that found in the *Xpantzay Cartulary*. This cartulary, written in Kaqchikel Maya, was presented by Xpantzay family members to the Spanish authorities in Guatemala in 1659 in an effort to regain ancestral lands (Maxwell and Hill 2006: 17 [Kaqchikel translations by these authors]). To validate the Xpantzays' claim on the land, the document links Xpantzay descendants to their earlier kin who held title to the land, referencing events that may first have been recorded on "precontact cartographic histories" (18). Using the subsection "Wars of the Sotz'il and Tuquche'," in particular,

Xpantzay claimants tie themselves by kinship to the earlier lords of the land that engaged in different battles (658–91), and it is here that we see a person take ossified form.

The "Wars of the Sotz'il and Tuquche'" relates how the son of a lord seeks to attack an important city, Koja'. Trying to stir up his warriors to attack this city, K'iqab', who reigned in the fifteenth century, exclaims, "The bones of my father are still there at Koja'. He has become their slave" (676). K'iqab' speaks of how his father's fingers and toes "are used as dice; his skull is cleaned; his bones have become arms of their thread winders." K'iqab' sees this use of his father's bones as no less than the manipulation of his living father himself. After successfully appealing to his warriors to end these indignities and go sack the city, K'iqab' "brought back the bones of his father from Koja'" (683), freeing him from his captors.[1] This action emboldens K'iqab' to sack additional cities and extend his influence in his ossified father's name.

These passages show that curated bones materialized the selves of important people, something done to either continue subduing enemy persons, or to continue extolling illustrious individuals long after their death. The current staging of the *Rabinal Achi* dance in Guatemala also shows this (Tedlock 2003). When Cawek beholds the calabash-envisioned-as-skull, reflects aloud about his arm bone, and then links them to his father and to his own future, he is not simply tying bone to specific bodies. He is inscribing the bone with the living memory of his progenitor and tying it to his own future (266–67). Similarly, when lord K'iqab' repatriates his father's bones he pays witness to an ancestral grandeur that propels him to great deeds (Maxwell and Hill 2006: 676). The quality of bone as enduring testaments to not only an individual's greatness, but also the ancestral core of his identity is clearly asserted in these Maya texts.

We find another dramatic instance in which personal identities literally ossify into human bone in the colonial era K'iche' Maya document, *Pop Wuj*. Modern editions of this work are based on what Fray Francisco Ximénez copied from an earlier text between 1701 and 1703 (Sam Colop 2012: xvii; Tedlock 1985: 23–24), but the age and form of this earlier text are unknown. References in the Ximénez copy suggest that it or its mid-sixteenth-century precursor, now lost, may have been pictographic (Sam Colop 2012: xii, xv; Tedlock 1985: 30–32), linking it to preceding Post-classic- and Classic-era formats used for recording and transmitting ideas. In a key *Pop Wuj* episode, the maiden Xquic approaches a calabash tree where the skull of the sacrificed Hun Hunahpu has been placed. Hun Hunahpu's skull, called "bak," bone, in the K'iche' document (Villacorta C. and Rodas N. 1927: 224), spits into Xquic's hand and tells her she has received his descendants. She becomes pregnant with the twins Hunahpu and Xbalanque who set out to avenge their father's and uncle's death. As part of their plan to destroy the Lords of Xibalba, the twins immolate themselves and arrange to have their bones ground up and thrown into a river. From these ground bones arise the twins in their new form, who defeat death (Recinos, Goetz, and Morley 1972: 117–64). Colonial K'iche' Mayas again convey compellingly how they concentrate self in bone.

The K'iche' Maya *Pop Wuj* is not alone in aligning the human skull with personal and ancestral selves, though. As William N. Duncan and Charles Hofling (2011) argue from examining current Maya practices of ritual head protection, Classic Mayas also may have viewed the skull, especially the shaped skull, as housing a person's spiritual essence. When considered with Hun Hunahpu's spitting action in the *Pop Wuj*, Duncan and Hofling's (2011) argument also raises the possibility that spittle, like the skull it issues from, is likewise tied to spiritual essence and to some form of ancestral continuity.

The three colonial Maya documents of Guatemala spotlight bone as the locus of individuated personal forces, a view of bone expressed also by Yucatec Mayas of northeastern Mexico during the colonial era. The degree to which Yucatecs recognized self in bone is in fact revealing of how different Maya groups held congruent belief systems. To this effect, the *Relación de las cosas de Yucatán* (ca. 1566) documents different ways that sixteenth-century Yucatec Mayas manipulated bone to either revere certain individuals or mark their defeat or capture. The *Relación*'s author(s) recounts(s), for example, how Yucatec Mayas would keep the skulls of certain dead lords, saw off their back part, reconstruct them with bitumen, and venerate them (Tozzer [1941] 1966: 131). This report, together with the many interred Classic Maya skeletons found with faces and/or heads removed (Morley, Brainerd, and J. Sharer 1983: 244–45; Ricketson and Ricketson 1937: plates 48a, 48b), bolsters the likelihood that Mayas of the Classic and Postclassic also venerated individuals using skulls like these. Moreover, with the *Relación*'s reporting of colonial-period Yucatec warriors who, "after (a) victory . . . took the jaws off the dead bodies and with the flesh cleaned off, . . . put them on their arms" (Tozzer [1941] 1966: 123), we witness how Yucatecs embodied captives, also, using curated bones of the skull.[2] This applied both to vanquished enemies and to slaves that had been captured in war and later sacrificed. The masters would display the slaves' bones in special dances, "as tokens of victory," perhaps marking their capture (Tozzer [1941] 1966: 120). The slaves' identities are here locked into the bones and made available through the bones to those who wanted to brandish them. Colonial-period Mayas of Yucatan deployed these practices, importantly, within a framework of bone use shared by colonial-era Mayas in Guatemala, and traceable to Postclassic and earlier complexes.

## Bones and Venerated Selves in the Classic period

The ways that Mayas handle bones in these colonial documents draw from Postclassic Maya outlooks and constitute latter-day expressions of Classic-era practices of Maya ancestor veneration. Classic Mayas linked human skeletal remains to enduring personal forces and used bones to support claims of ancestry to specific people. Many examples of this feature in archaeological settings, especially in secondary burials and in the curation of individual bones (Scherer 2015). A closer look at how Classic Mayas put bones to these uses can deepen our understanding of how they imprinted identity on bones and of why Postclassic- and colonial-era Mayas continued to recognize many ritual potencies in bones. During the Classic period, Mayas showed a strong interest in venerating and revering certain dead individuals. Archaeologists routinely find human remains that have been carefully interred in different parts of Classic Maya sites, buttressing the idea that the inhabitants of those places wanted to commemorate past individuals and link themselves personally to them. The ways these Mayas handled human remains suggests they were operating within an established framework of ancestor veneration, and that they were actively trying to immortalize certain dead individuals. Archaeological findings suggest that Classic Mayas went to great lengths to materialize the self of some illustrious dead and to use them as needed.

Part of how they did this can be seen in the many ways Mayas buried their dead and handled their skeletons. Scholars have pointed out how many Classic Maya burials show evidence of multiple entries and manipulation of bones. David Webster (1997: 6), for instance, notes that tombs were routinely reopened and bones were retrieved, in many cases reburied elsewhere. Like at other places, the interaction between the living and the dead at Chan, Belize, in the Mid-Late and Terminal Classic involved "removal and redeposition of skulls" and "reuse of grave space for secondary burials" (Novotny 2014: 60). That postmortem practices like these were intended to venerate important persons is affirmed by Andrea Cucina and Vera Tiesler (2014: 228), who state that, "treatments, like cremation, postdepositional burning, extraction (reduction) or addition of corpses, and reuse and recycling (of the body, the skeleton, or its segments), have all been clearly identified as ancestral behaviors." When Classic Mayas extracted bones from burials, it was very often to curate those bones as part of a larger ancestral cult. For them, "Single bones of ancestors as relics were often destined to be venerated in temples and altars or to accompany later primary interments of family members" (228). They would sometimes safeguard bones to preserve a material manifestation of their forebears or other eminent dead and to link these to their own mortal remains. W. B. M. Welsh (1988: 186–201), meanwhile, emphasizes that skeletons evidence ancestor veneration not only by the physical state in which they are found, but via their interment in relation to domestic space. Building on this line of thinking, Arlen Chase and Diane Z. Chase (1994: 56) argue that the Classic-era veneration of the dead at Caracol can also be surmised by the placement of the dead near eastern buildings and plaza spaces, locations associated with the reborn sun.

Taking into account cases like these, as well as their own work on Maya interments, Cucina and Tiesler (2014: 246) encourage us to think less about single burial events and more about "mortuary programs" that involve complex handling and redeposition of bone. They and others have documented funerary depositions in caves that may also have been part of these kinds of programs (Cucina and Tiesler 2014: 226; Glassman and Bonor Villarejo 2005: 289), enlarging our view of how the skeletal depositions that archaeologists find represent punctuations in a succession of site-specific events, rather than the end points of ritual activity. As Chase and Chase (1994: 58) put it with respect to Caracol, "Tombs were…utilized as non-final resting places." At any point in a tomb's history its inhabitants could be called on to serve a pressing need.

In different contexts, the postmortem handling of bones pays witness to the need to link oneself to illustrious individuals, even if those individuals were not related by lineal descent (McAnany 1995: 131; see Astor-Aguilera 2010: 34, 165). Patricia A. McAnany (1995: 161) refers to ancestors as specific dead individuals who were important for legitimizing access to resources for specific groups. Persons claiming elite status and rulership had the most at stake when trying to link themselves to the right ancestors, so they probably went to great lengths to justify their claims, including engaging in practices like bloodletting (Freidel, Schele, and Parker 1993: 205; Kremer and Uc Flores 1996: 87). The veneration of dynastically important ancestors played a key role in the elaboration of social hierarchy that culminated in the Late Classic (600–900 CE) (Tiesler and Cucina 2010: 94). Nowhere do we see this in more relief than Palenque, where enormous efforts were made to commemorate and preserve the remains of the city's most illustrious ruler, Pakal (Ruz Lluillier 1965). Where dynastic interests played out, ritualizing connections to a ruler could bestow legitimacy to claims of rulership by successors. This was also a major concern among the successors of the Copan ruler, Yax K'uk Mo', who linked themselves to this founding ancestor (Stuart 2004: 215). That his dynastic line ran through fifteen later rulers of the city attests to the resoluteness with which his claimed descendants held sway.

It also attests to how, on a wider scale, Classic Mayas were able to imprint personal identities on objects and use these objects to justify successions. Stephen Houston, David Stuart, and Karl Taube (2006: 11) have argued that during the Maya Classic, "portraits contained part of the royal essence" of rulers, and that rulers' "essences shifted into other materials, many enduring well beyond the decay of flesh." They related this to how, in iconography, Mayas used parts of the body to represent the whole individual (64). We are thus reminded that if Classic Mayas considered stone portraits to be imbued with royal essence and if they recognized whole individuals in their body parts then these Mayas were especially motivated to view the actual bones of past rulers as materializations of their royal selves.

Nevertheless, although the need to link oneself to an illustrious person was especially plausible where dynastic interests operated, the desire to assert ties to the deceased probably occurred on a smaller scale, too. The record suggests that an individual's identity could not only be innately tied to his or her own bones but that it could also be actively *inscribed* onto bones, including a person's own bones. In two Terminal Classic (750–1050 CE) cases, bones are made to reference specific individuals in a manner suggesting how those persons' identities were purposely anchored in those bones. One intricately carved femur, for example, was found in an Ek Balam burial, held in the decedent's left hand. It is glyphically inscribed with the name of the person whose bone it was, or perhaps the name of an ancestor of whom it was a relic. Another carved femur, found in a burial urn in Dzibilchaltun, seems to name the person to whom the bone belonged (Grube, Lacadena, and Martin 2003: 25, 33–34).

In other cases, while Mayas may not have inscribed personal names onto bones, they applied great care when crafting objects out of individual bones. The efforts they put to carving specific bones are suggestive of how they recognized individuated personal forces in curated bone, and supports the possibility that at least some bone objects found in Late Classic and Postclassic interments were thought by their handlers to house such personal forces. Carved human bones like those found at Late Classic Baking Pot, Belize, and at Postclassic Iximche', Guatemala, point to this recognition. Among the artifacts recovered at Baking Pot was a bowl carved from a Late-Classic cranium, one featuring a deliberately flattened base (Ricketson 1929: 14). At Iximche', meanwhile, excavators recovered a pentatonic flute made from a child's femur and a bracelet carved from an adult occipital bone (Guillemin 1965: 31–33, 51). While these objects take recognizable forms as usable objects, they may have been more than just instruments and adornments. They may have forged organic ties to the individuals the bones came from, to the point that they could anchor and even imprison a person's identity, availing the possessor of the objects with the deceased person's vital essence and with some control over them. What could have made these erstwhile use-objects still more compelling as materialized selves is the fact that they were not only made from human bone, but that they were *recognizably* made from human bone. Just enough of the original bone may have been left in the object to let others know it was of human origin, to remind the beholder of its source.[3] Curated bone objects, carved or otherwise, could thus forcefully attest to the individual held captive through their former body part.

But a related interpretation of "captivity" by bone is also possible. Referring to Maya Classic-period examples, Houston, Stuart, and Taube (2006: 72) have suggested that the possession of bones by a warrior can indicate the actual absorbing of the dead captive's identity by the captor. This makes it possible to view bone, as James L. Fitzsimmons (2011: 58) argues, not only as a locus of identity but also as a vehicle of identity transfer. The principle of controlling and even absorbing identity appears in the cases above and is quite plausible in the captive-bone episodes found in the *Rabinal Achi* and the *Xpantzay Cartulary*. The way the Classic Maya *baak* or *b'aak* (bone) can be read as captive in Classic-era inscriptions (Houston, Stuart, and Taube 2006: 64, 221; Scherer 2015: 102) helps elucidate these cases of bone manipulation, instances that showcase bone as a vehicle of subjugation. *Baq*'s cognates continue bearing the dual meanings of "bone" and "captive" in different Maya languages today (Burdick 2010: 124), underlining the need to keep both meanings in mind when reading colonial Maya manuscripts.

Still, while Classic Mayas handled the skeletal remains of specific people to exert dominance over them, they also handled specific people's bones when they wished to pay them respect, to emulate them, and to draw from the sacred strength they showed in life. Aligning themselves with the distinguished dead might also link them to the dead's capacity for continued existence. To this point, when examining mortuary practices from Formative (2000 BCE–200 CE) to Postclassic Chan, Belize, Anna C. Novotny (2014: 61) argues that, "Human bone represented important tenets of Maya worldview: cyclical regeneration and renewal." From at least the Classic period, then, the ancestor cult with its postmortem handling of bones was likely motivated by abiding concerns for renewal. Individuals needing to cement their continuity with certain people and wanting to tap into their enduring essence found bones an effective way of doing this on through the Postclassic period, and likely into the colonial period. But these ways of investing bones with meaning appear to have changed from the colonial period to the present day. Evidence suggests that, since the colonial era, Mayas moved away from identifying bones with named individuals and instead came to emphasize other, related qualities of bone, some with more immediate importance.

### Shifting Usages of Bone

Studies from the last one hundred years have shown that while Mayas are still interested in materializing selves and in interacting with selves manifested in bone, this interest is undergoing change in different Maya groups. Two examples are illustrative. Itza' Mayas of San José Petén, Guatemala, for instance, venerate three curated skulls as part of their yearly devotions, and every year on the night of 1 November, one of three old skulls is taken from a church to some homes whose owners have invited it (Reina 1962: 31–32). They receive the skull as an esteemed guest, and its arrival at the homes coincides with the arrival of deceased relatives. It is then returned to the church around sunrise. In the Lacandon Maya cultural complex, meanwhile, the gods must be venerated and fed in cave shrines containing incense burners, incense vessels, and human bones and skulls. The bones located around Lake Mensabak, Chiapas, are considered to be "the remains of gods who at one time took human form" (McGee 1990: 57), and they receive prayers and copal incense. Lacandons also view them as their forebears who had to "stand before the gods" and attend to them in their lakeside homes (Cucina, Tiesler, Palka 2015: 159, 162). But while ritual practices have been carried out in the rock shelters since colonial, and possibly Postclassic, days (Cucina et al. 2012: 42), the rock shelters have received less ritual attention in the last few generations.

In both these cases, Mayas are handling human bones in the process of honoring a class of beings. However, the materialization of self, with ties to specific ancestrality, is occurring in a much more diffuse way. It is not focused on named humans or on specific ancestors. Among the Itza' the link between the bones and the humans they once belonged to has become especially tenuous. The actual identity of the skulls has been lost (Reina 1962: 31). And while Lacandons do tie bones in rock shelters to the ancestral past, they view the original owners of the bones as having had a primarily godly identity when they walked the earth, as R. Jon McGee (1990: 57) notes above. They are not addressed by individual names, only as a class: "caretakers of the gods" (Cucina et al. 2012: 42). Their role as sacred caretakers stands above that of ancestors. These cases mark a clear departure from the way Classic Mayas (Chase and Chase 1994) and Postclassic Mayas (Sigal 2000: 145–46) placed a premium on linking their personal history with revered individuals, and on being able to name them (McAnany 1995: 49).

Still, even as we note an attenuation of ancestral emphasis in Maya ethnographic contexts of the last several decades, we can identify a more pronounced interest in the regenerative and fertility aspects of bone in the region.[4] In the Q'eqchi' Maya *k'ajb'ak*, a "bone splintering" ritual, for instance, Guatemalan Q'eqchi's perform acts of abstinence thirteen days before and after the maize planting for renewal and fertility (Pop 2000: 22). The "bone splintering" references the body being cleansed and subordinated for the common good. K'iche' Mayas of Momostenango, Guatemala, meanwhile, take human bones from the cemetery to place in a local San Simón effigy. The bones are installed "at the base of the throat or where the top of the sternum would be." According to the owner of the shrine where the effigy is kept, "This helps it to call the nawales" (Cook and Offit 2013: 148). It also enables it to grant good or evil petitions. This bone placement will "activate the power of the image" (148), making it a key interlocutor between humans and nawales, the earth lords on whom K'iche's depend for plentiful harvests and good health. Farther south in Guatemala we find that Tz'utujiil Mayas refer to maize seeds they will plant as *jolooma*, "little skulls." These seeds/skulls will germinate into new maize plants and new seeds (Carlsen 1997: 54). The way these Mayas handle bones (and talk about bones) appears increasingly motivated by ideas of regeneration and renewal, and less by ideas about ancestors.

Instances like these underscore how people in local communities tie older understandings of bone as a repository for spiritual essence (Astor-Aguilera 2010: 172–75; López Austin 1980 2:177) to strategies for ensuring local bounty. Bone promotes agricultural fertility through the literal and figurative ways that Mayas handle it. Its ceremonial treatment furthers this not only by renewing the personal and social body and preparing it for blessings from earth lords, but by clearing the channels of communication between Mayas and these earth lords in the first place. Together with other seasonal activities meant to ensure good plantings, practices centered on human bone reveal a substrate of agricultural life deeply embedded in multigenerational ties to the land. The ways Mayas like these use bone in contexts of fertility and regeneration help frame how another group of twentieth- and early twenty-first century Mayas is also harnessing the potentialities of bone, especially its diagnostic and therapeutic properties.

## Current Maya Bonesetting and Instrumental Uses of Bone

Maya bone healers working in highland Guatemala evidence two things: one, that Mayas today take bone injuries very seriously, and two, that a group of Maya healers that treats bone and handles bones ritually is mainly concerned with the instrumental uses of bone and not with ancestral uses. Bonesetters of San Pedro La Laguna are quite revealing in this regard. They view bones (living bones, excarnate bones, and surrogate bones) in practical and ritually charged ways but without any ancestral connotations. Their work marks a further shift away from privileging an ancestral view of bones, and more toward viewing bones as having chiefly instrumental importance. That they ritualize some of their approach to bonesetting is also noteworthy because throughout Mesoamerica bonesetting takes mostly secular, nonritual forms (Hinojosa 2002: 29–30; Paul and McMahon 2001: 243). In most of the region, the need to handle bones in pragmatic ways outweighs other considerations. The San Pedro La Laguna case thus illustrates that even in a bonesetting tradition that exhibits an atypically ritualized view of bones it does not regard bones ancestrally.

During fieldwork in San Pedro La Laguna and neighboring towns, conducted during several stays between 1998 and 2002, I interacted with ten Tz'utujiil Maya bonesetters. I observed three of the bonesetters as they treated clients who came to their homes, and two bonesetters as they did rounds in town and treated clients in a nearby community. I interviewed the remaining bonesetters in their homes. In all instances my manner of learning was by observing, asking questions, and taking notes. It quickly became apparent that though these bonesetters use their hands extensively to diagnose and treat bodily injuries, they use more than just their hands. Among Maya bonesetters, San Pedro–area bonesetters are unique in that they also use some found objects. As Francisco Rodríguez Rouanet (1969) and Benjamin D. Paul (1976) first reported, San Pedro bonesetters locate objects that enable them to work, and whose appearance seemingly endorses them in their work. They call these objects *baq* or *hueso* ("bone"). Baq can take different forms, like the vertebrae of small mammals and snakes, flat river stones, and pre-Columbian lithics. Whatever they look like, the baq are revealed sacra, yielded up by the earth lords and imbued with quite unique potentialities.

Local bonesetters report that baq have penetrative, almost magnetic powers that allow them to detect irregularities in living human bones, like fractures and dislocations. When the bonesetter takes the baq in his hand and applies it to the client's injury site, the baq is said to move about on its own. It will move differently depending on the injury, bonesetters say, and it can even therapeutically move bones inside the body. One anthropologist who worked in Santiago Atitlán remarked that the best-known baq ever in San Pedro La Laguna might have been of human origin, a quality that could account for this object's ability to relay much information about sufferers' bodies (Douglas 1969: 144). But its human origin furthered its healing efficacy and potency, and not any ancestral authority. It is revealing that San Pedro–area bonesetters have come to use the term *baq* to refer to a range of non-bone objects that they bring into their work. *Baq* is referring less and less to bone in a literal way, and more to bone in an instrumental manner. Bonesetters are so invested in instrumentalized bones that they regularly find bones and use them in surrogate form. They usually keep an assemblage of these near their home altars, and always keep one on their person in case they have to treat someone away from home.

The unique Bones and bone healing are under the dominion of a particular guardian who sometimes appears in revelatory dreams to locals (Hinojosa 2004: 115) when he might instruct certain people in how to use the found baq to heal (Paul and McMahon 2001: 249). The sacred quality of bone in living human bodies is such that revealed baq should be handled only by people with the ritual authority to do so. For this reason, it is well-known whether specific local bonesetters have received divine election through their dreams and through finding a baq in the hills; townspeople talk about this. In this subset of Tz'utujiil Maya bonesetters, then, we can observe yet more attenuation of linkages between bones and ancestrality. We instead see bonesetters applying the sacred instrumental quality of baq in their work. The physical urgency of bonesetting requires them to leverage the ritual potentiality of bone and its surrogates to help the injured. An analogous instrumental quality of bone appears in other Maya contexts in the early twentieth century, I should add. Morris Steggerda and Barbara Korsch (1943: 55), for example, reported that a Yucatec Maya healer in Mexico would take a tooth from a human skeleton and rub it against the tooth of someone with a toothache to relieve the pain. The tooth's potency was wholly instrumental, a property of bone that extends to nonhuman bone, too: Yucatec healers have also used crocodile teeth and deer antlers to treat toothache (Roys [1931] 1976: 186, 188, 191).

The unique potentialities of bone can thus take different forms. They can even manifest in more daunting ways, creating a fear reaction among some Mayas. For example, even though Tzotzil Mayas of Chiapas are very interested in their ancestral deities (Vogt 1976: 16), they altogether avoid human bone remains (Holland 1962: 215). Bones have become dangerously powerful for them, in a way concurring with what Hernán García, Antonio Sierra, and Gilberto Balám (1999) report about Yucatec Mayas.

Among Yucatec Mayas, stone burial mounds called *kuyos* can produce many illnesses "because the bones of the dead are gathered there, and because the aluxob live there protecting the remains" (247). The aluxob send potentially harmful winds from the burial mounds. Mayas of these two groups feel that the deceased's bones can afflict people with illness, and so must be avoided. This aversion to bones emphatically suggests that bones are not an appropriate vehicle or conduit for accessing the ancestors, perhaps because the bones' magical potentiality may now be tied to beings other than their original human owners.

These expressions of fear about bones may be hard to square with how many Mayas do spend time in cemeteries remembering and feeding their dead. Clearly not all Mayas feel imperiled by bones, but the fact that some do may be related to how many Mayas today address ancestors in a generalized, collective way, and not by emphasizing personal bonds to named people from the distant past (McAnany 1995: 30). When highland Guatemala Mayas speak of their ancestors (aside from deceased close relatives), they more often speak of them in terms of undifferentiated *abuelos* or *antepasados* than in terms of specific illustrious individuals (Hinojosa 2015: 65). This is reflected in the formalized way Kaqchikel Mayas invoke *qati't qamama'*, "our grandmothers, our grandfathers," when talking about their forebears. Kaqchikels of San Juan Comalapa will sooner name a prominent town citizen of the past (like artists, composers, and politicians) than identify prominent personal ancestors. Similarly, among Tz'utujiils, the ancestral beings that count are the originary *nawal acha*, the ancient ones that engendered the present order and who are replaced in their turn (Stanzione 2003: 58). The nonnaming of long-deceased people in invocations reflects a general de-emphasis on specific ancestry. It also correlates with how, in cases in which Mayas do associate ancestors somewhat with bones, those Mayas do not stress the need to continuously handle the bones of specific people, or even bones in general, when invoking the dead.

K'iche' Mayas, to this point, invoke the dead collectively when making ritual petitions. But though they do not outright fear bones, neither do they seek bones out as a first-line conduit of invocation when prefacing their work with prayers to the dead. In Garrett W. Cook and Thomas A. Offit's (2013) study of ritual in Momostenango, they report that when a ritualist and his group were going to invoke the dead, they first went to the chapel called *calvario*, but finding it closed, they *then* went to the cemetery's ossuary. Significantly, although the ossuary can help access the "common souls of the dead" (69), it is secondary in this respect to the calvario chapel. Even the ossuary's bone-filled interior does not make it the preferred site for accessing the dead. It is not necessary to invoke the dead using the bones of the dead, something evident among Yucatec Mayas as well.

Yucatec Mayas handle specific skeletons to bring about pragmatic ends, but bones are not altogether necessary for this either. In remote villages of Quintana Roo, some Yucatec Mayas exhume a person's skull and long bones three to five years after burial (Astor-Aguilera 2010: 159). Once they have been cleaned, wrapped, and fed, the mortuary bundle is brought home. If the bundle has been properly prepared, it can enable people to communicate with an ancestor (163). But the spiritual beings tethered to mortuary bundles have feisty temperaments and can become hard to control; people must exercise caution around them, even as they petition them for help. Surrogates for the bone bundle can be made and activated, though, and these are often kept in the home while the actual bones are returned to the cemetery (162–63). So while some Yucatecs initiate contact with ancestors through their bones, many find this to be too problematic and prefer to use bone surrogates rather than the bones themselves.

As these cases show, bone can encase principles ranging from useful to pernicious. But though in Momostenango bone has been seen less as a site where self materializes and more as a site of ritual potentialities (Cook and Offit 2013), this is only partly the case elsewhere. Inhabitants of Quintana Roo keep more linkages in place between bone and ancestry, but this is tempered by anxieties about the magical powers of mortuary bundles containing exhumed bones (Astor-Aguilera 2010). Yucatecs there fear what powers the bones can unleash, especially through harmful winds, and through the people who can wield these powers (169). They emphasize using and managing these forces to achieve certain ends, and do not emphasize tying themselves publicly to a forebear. Mayas are increasingly seeing bones and boneyards as sites of ritual potentialities and less as the material residue of their progenitors.

In line with this, human bones, whether buried or in bundles, are thought by some contemporary Mayas to harbor many dangers and are avoided. Their dangerous potentialities seemingly outweigh any ancestral qualities they might still contain and that Mayas of the colonial era and earlier periods recognized. Even Mayas today without an outright fear of bones still keep a cautious, respectful stance around them. To do otherwise could expose them to the risky potencies of bone that raise so much worry in local communities (García, Sierra, and Balám 1999: 247). But when the powers of bone and bone surrogates get harnessed by those who are authorized to do so, like San Pedro La Laguna bonesetters, they can communicate deep information about living bones in the body, and even guide a healer's hands (Hinojosa 2004: 115). Wherever these Maya bonesetters work, they use bone and its surrogates to accomplish specific tasks, suggesting a ritual pliability of bone that has morphed significantly since the time that Classic-era Mayas attributed great ancestral importance to these body parts.

Based on archaeological and documentary evidence, Classic-, Post-classic-, and colonial-era Mayas clearly used bones to materialize important selves and to manipulate them as captives. They imprinted identity on bone, making it available for venerating forebears and for controlling adversaries. This property of bone contextualizes how different personages took ossified form in the colonial documents *Rabinal Achi*, *Xpantzay Cartulary*, and *Pop Wuj*. It enabled enemy actors to capture Maya potentates in pars pro toto fashion, hold them captive, and possibly absorb their strength, particularly in the first two of these documents. The synonymy between "bone" and "captive" in Maya languages thus signals the unique capacity of bone for anchoring and ultimately controlling specific selves. It is all the more significant, then, that while upholding the view that bones remain imbued with strong potentialities, Mayas have since the colonial era de-emphasized bone's capacity for encasing specific selves. They have given less weight to the idea of bones as a concentration of a person's qualities and identity, and have come to view bones more as objects with instrumental potential, as exemplified by how Tz'utujiil Maya bonesetters use bones.

## Conclusions

From at least as early as the Classic period, Mayas have used excarnate human bones to validate ties between generations. Through the succeeding Postclassic period and into the colonial era Mayas continued connecting bones, perhaps because of their palpable immediacy and hardness, to enduring personal forces and used them to support claims of ancestry. They handled specific bones and fashioned them into objects because they wanted to ossify, and thus venerate or control, the persons the bones came from. Colonial documents from Guatemala likewise pay witness to how bones anchored important selves and even seeded future human life. But as twentieth-century and later ethnographic accounts suggest, the link between bones and specific ancestrality has diminished. We no longer see Mayas stress ancestry via bone to the degree suggested by documentary and archaeological evidence from the colonial era and earlier periods. Still, the fact that colonial, Postclassic, and Classic Mayas recognized bones as objects housing residues of their former owners helps elucidate how Mayas of more recent decades retain the idea that certain ritual potentialities are anchored in bone, even if these potentialities are not understood chiefly in terms of ossified ancestral selves. Mayas in the ethnographic record regard bones in instrumental ways, capturing a view of bone that, while suggesting concerns with regeneration and fertility, does not emphasize specific ancestors. Still, by putting bones to instrumental uses, many contemporary Mayas are mapping onto existing frameworks that attribute unique potentialities to bone. Guatemalan Tz'utujiil Maya bonesetters are among those who recognize sacred, instrumental qualities in bone and who put these qualities to pragmatic use. Like many other Mayas, today Tz'utujiil Maya bonesetters value the immediate practical utility of bone over its ties to specific people. In line with this tendency, concerns about ancestry that can still be identified among Mayas of the last several decades have moved away from a primary association with bone. The ancestors still command respect, but this respect has taken more collective form, and one not primarily tethered to their material remains.

To the extent that Maya views about bone are changing, though, it would be premature to say that this marks a permanent shift in thinking, or that it rules out the possibility that Mayas think about bone in terms of ancestrality and sacred instrumentality at the same time. Brian Stross (2007) advanced the view that bone can simultaneously encase qualities of materialized self and sacred instrumentality, suggesting that one need not preclude the other. While this may be true, it is clear that Mayas have increasingly diminished the connection between bone and individuated self, and have instead deployed the instrumental powers of bone, to the point that Tz'utujiil Maya bonesetters today rely on bone and bone surrogates for their work. Given this, just why Tz'utujiil Maya bonesetters have come to use sacred bones in their therapeutics whereas other Maya bonesetters have not merits further exploration. By establishing that bones remain culturally pliable and responsive to different needs, this study brings us closer to a native model of bone use and suggests that Maya ideas not only inform a range of activities, but also inhabit material objects.

## Notes

I am grateful to Rebecca Dufendach for her many efforts in assembling this issue and to *Ethnohistory* editor John F. Schwaller for arranging the reviews of its component articles, including my own. My sincere appreciation goes to the anonymous reader for his or her invaluable feedback on an earlier version of this article. All translations are my own unless otherwise noted.

1  Davide Domenici (2017: 499) reaffirms this view of bone as a trophy captive in sixteenth-century central Mexico, reporting that two human bones in an artifact inventory were "body parts of a king captured and sacrificed."
2  Signaling how this view of bone was present in other parts of Mesoamerica, Postclassic Nahuas curated the femur of an enemy warrior, calling it the *malteutl*, the "god captive" (Sahagún 1981: 60).
3  Objects for apparent rasping or musical use, and clearly made from human bones, are well-known from central Mexico (Beyer 1934: 334–44; Domenici 2017: 498, 506; von Winning 1959: 88).

4 Ethnographic cases outside the Maya area reveal how bones contain powers of regeneration and healing. Otomis, for instance, mark out bones as vehicles of sacred power and fertility (Galinier 2004: 102, 197). They link bones with life energy and ancestrality, and designate bone marrow as the source of both sperm and blood (197–98). The energetic quality of bone even makes ground bone useful in vitalistic potions (102). Otomi bone rituals are ultimately meant to bring fertility to the earth. This recalls how in colonial Mexico, ground-up human bones were assigned the power of sexual attraction (Aguirre Beltrán 1963: 174). A Nahua healer of the mid-twentieth century, meanwhile, recognized the instrumental qualities of bone in curing, using ancient bones to treat fright sickness (Madsen 1960: 69).

# References

Aguirre Beltrán, Gonzalo. 1963. *Medicina y magia: El proceso de aculturación en la estructura colonial.* Mexico City: Instituto Nacional Indigenista.

Astor-Aguilera, Miguel Angel. 2010. *The Maya World of Communicating Objects: Quadripartite Crosses, Trees, and Stones.* Albuquerque: University of New Mexico Press.

Axtell, James. 1979. "Ethnohistory: An Historian's Viewpoint." *Ethnohistory* 26, no. 1: 1–13.

Beyer, Hermann. 1934. "Mexican Bone Rattles." *Middle American Pamphlet No. 7 of Publication No. 5*, 321–49. New Orleans: Department of Middle American Research, Tulane University.

Burdick, Catherine Elizabeth. 2010. "Text and Image in Classic Maya Sculpture: A.D. 600–900." PhD diss., University of Illinois at Chicago.

Cardoza y Aragón, Luis. 1972. *Rabinal-Achí: El varón de Rabinal.* Mexico City: Porrúa, S. A.

Carlsen, Robert S. 1997. *The War for the Heart and Soul of a Highland Maya Town.* Austin: University of Texas Press.

Chase, Arlen, and Diane Z. Chase. 1994. "Maya Veneration of the Dead at Caracol, Belize." In *Seventh Palenque Round Table, 1989*, edited by Merle G. Robertson and Virginia M. Fields, 55–62. San Francisco: Pre-Columbian Art Research Institute.

Cook, Garrett W., and Thomas A. Offit. 2013. *Indigenous Religion and Cultural Performance in the New Maya World.* Albuquerque: University of New Mexico Press.

Cucina, Andrea, and Vera Tiesler. 2014. "Mortuary Pathways and Ritual Meanings Related to Maya Human Bone Deposits in Subterranean Contexts." In *The Bioarchaeology of Space and Place: Ideology, Power, and Meaning in Maya Mortuary Contexts*, edited by Gabriel D. Wrobel, 225–54. New York: Springer.

Cucina, Andrea, Vera Tiesler, and Joel Palka. 2015. "The Identity and Worship of Human Remains in Rockshelter Shrines among the Northern Lacandons of Mensabak." *Estudios de Cultura Maya* 45: 141–69.

Cucina, Andrea, Vera Tiesler, Joel Palka, Julio R. Chi Keb, and Shintaro Suzuki. 2012. "Estudio tafonómico e bioarqueológico de los restos humanos de lacandones, enterrados en santuarios de Cueva de la Laguna Mensabak,

Chiapas." In *Memorias, XXI Encuentro Internacional, Los investigadores de la cultura maya, Tomo I*, 33–46. Campeche, Mexico: Universidad Autónoma de Campeche.

de León Valdés, Carlos Rolando, and Francisco López Perén. 1985. *Popol Vuh*. Guatemala City: Ministerio de Educación.

Domenici, Davide. 2017. "The *Descrittione dell'India occidentale*, a Sixteenth-Century Source on the Italian Reception of Mesoamerican Material Culture." *Ethnohistory* 64, no. 4: 497–527.

Douglas, Bill Gray. 1969. "Illness and Curing in Santiago Atitlan, a Tzutujil-Maya Community in the Southwestern Highlands of Guatemala." PhD diss., Stanford University.

Duncan, William N., and Charles Andrew Hofling. 2011. "Why the Head? Cranial Modification as Protection and Ensoulment among the Maya." *Ancient Mesoamerica* 22: 199–210.

Fenton, William N. 1962. "Ethnohistory and Its Problems." *Ethnohistory* 9, no. 1: 1–23.

Fitzsimmons, James L. 2011. "Perspectives on Death and Transformation in Ancient Maya Society." In *Living with the Dead: Mortuary Ritual in Mesoamerica*, edited by James L. Fitzsimmons and Izumi Shimada, 53–77. Tucson: University of Arizona Press.

Freidel, David, Linda Schele, and Joy Parker. 1993. *Maya Cosmos: Three Thousand Years on the Shaman's Path*. New York: William Morrow.

Galinier, Jacques. 2004. *The World Below: Body and Cosmos in Otomi Indian Ritual*. Boulder: University Press of Colorado.

García, Hernán, Antonio Sierra, and Gilberto Balám. 1999. *Wind in the Blood: Mayan Healing and Chinese Medicine*, translated by Jeff Conant. Berkeley, CA: North Atlantic.

Glassman, David M., and Juan Luis Bonor Villarejo. 2005. "Mortuary Practices of the Prehistoric Maya from Caves Branch Rock Shelter, Belize." In *Stone Houses and Earth Lords: Maya Religion in the Cave Context*, edited by Keith M. Prufer and James E. Brady, 285–96. Boulder: University Press of Colorado.

Grube, Nikolai, Alfonso Lacadena, and Simon Martin. 2003. "Chichén Itza and Ek Balam: Terminal Classic Inscriptions from Yucatan." In *Notebook for the Twenty-Seventh Maya Hieroglyphic Forum at Texas*, Part 2, edited by Nikolai Grube, 1–84. Austin, TX: Maya Workshop Foundation.

Guillemin, Jorge F. 1965. *Iximche': Capital del antiguo reino cakchiquel*. Guatemala City: Publicaciones del Instituto de Antropología e Historia de Guatemala.

Hinojosa, Servando Z. 2002. "'The Hands Know': Bodily Engagement and Medical Impasse in Highland Maya Bonesetting." *Medical Anthropology Quarterly* 16, no. 1: 22–40.

Hinojosa, Servando Z. 2004. "The Hands, the Sacred, and the Context of Change in Maya Bonesetting." In *Healing by Hand: Manual Medicine and Bonesetting in Global Perspective*, edited by Kathryn S. Oths and Servando Z. Hinojosa, 107–29. Walnut Creek, CA: AltaMira Press.

Hinojosa, Servando Z. 2015. *In this Body: Kaqchikel Maya and the Grounding of Spirit*. Albuquerque: University of New Mexico Press.

Holland, William R. 1962. "Highland Maya Folk Medicine: A Study of Culture Change." PhD diss., University of Arizona.

Houston, Stephen, David Stuart, and Karl Taube. 2006. *The Memory of Bones: Body, Being, and Experience among the Classic Maya*. Austin: University of Texas Press.

Kremer, Jurgen, and Fausto Uc Flores. 1996. "The Ritual Suicide of Maya Rulers." In *Eighth Palenque Round Table, 1993*, edited by Martha J. Macri and Jan McHargue, 79–91. Merle G. Robertson, ed. San Francisco: Pre-Columbian Art Research Institute. www.mesoweb.com/pari/publications/rt10/suicide.pdf (accessed 16 September 2015).

López Austin, Alfredo. 1980. *Cuerpo humano e ideología: Las concepciones de los antiguos Nahuas*. 2 vols. Mexico City: Universidad Nacional Autónoma de México.

Madsen, William. 1960. *The Virgin's Children: Life in an Aztec Village Today*. Austin: University of Texas Press.

Maxwell, Judith M., and Robert M. Hill II. 2006. *Kaqchikel Chronicles: The Definitive Edition*. Austin: University of Texas Press.

McAnany, Patricia A. 1995. *Living with the Ancestors: Kinship and Kingship in Ancient Maya Society*. Austin: University of Texas Press.

McGee, R. Jon. 1990. *Life, Ritual, and Religion among the Lacandon Maya*. Belmont, CA: Wadsworth.

Morley, Sylvanus G., George W. Brainerd, and Robert J. Sharer. 1983. *The Ancient Maya*. 4th ed. Stanford, CA: Stanford University Press.

Novotny, Anna C. 2014. "The Bones of the Ancestors as Inalienable Possessions: A Bioarchaeological Perspective." *Archeological Papers of the American Anthropological Association* 23, no. 1: 54–65.

Paul, Benjamin D. 1976. "The Maya Bonesetter as Sacred Specialist." *Ethnology* 15, no. 1: 77–81.

Paul, Benjamin D., and Clancy McMahon. 2001. "Mesoamerican Bonesetters." In *Mesoamerican Healers*, edited by Brad E. Huber and Alan R. Sandstrom, 243–69. Austin: University of Texas Press.

Pop, Hamilton. 2000. "Experiencia de uso de la tierra y producción." In *Tierra y espiritualidad maya. II encuentro taller sobre "cultura y espiritualidad maya," Guatemala, 14–17 febrero 2000*, 21–38. Cobán and Guatemala City: Ak'Kutan and Voces del Tiempo.

Recinos, Adrian, Delia Goetz, and Sylvanus G. Morley. 1972. *Popol Vuh: The Sacred Book of the Ancient Quiché Maya*. Norman: University of Oklahoma Press.

Reina, Ruben E. 1962. "The Ritual of the Skull in Petén, Guatemala." *Expedition* 4, no. 4: 27–35.

Ricketson Jr., Oliver. 1929. "Excavations at Baking Pot, British Honduras." *Contributions to American Archaeology*, no. 1: 1–27. Preprint from Publication no. 403. Washington, DC: Carnegie Institution of Washington.

Ricketson, Oliver G., and Edith Bayles Ricketson. 1937. *Uaxactun, Guatemala: Group E — 1926–1931*. Washington, DC: Carnegie Institution of Washington.

Rodríguez Rouanet, Francisco. 1969. "Prácticas médicas tradicionales de los indígenas de Guatemala." *Guatemala Indígena* 4, no. 2: 51–86.

Roys, Ralph L. (1931) 1976. *The Ethno-Botany of the Maya*. Department of Middle American Research, Pub. 2. New Orleans: Tulane University.

Ruz Lluillier, Alberto. 1965. "Tombs and Funerary Practices in the Maya Lowlands." In *Archaeology of Southern Mesoamerica, Part 1*. Vol. 2 of *Handbook of Middle American Indians*, edited by Gordon R. Willey, 441–61. Robert Wauchope, ed. Austin: University of Texas Press.

Sahagún, Bernardino de. 1981. *Florentine Codex: General History of the Things of New Spain. Book 2, The Ceremonies*, edited by Arthur J. O. Anderson and Charles E. Dibble. Santa Fe: School of American Research.

Sam Colop, Luis Enrique. 2012. *Popol Vuh*. Guatemala City: F&G.

Scherer, Andrew K. 2015. *Mortuary Landscapes of the Classic Maya: Rituals of Body and Soul*. Austin: University of Texas Press.

Sigal, Pete. 2000. *From Moon Goddesses to Virgins: The Colonization of Yucatecan Maya Sexual Desire*. Austin: University of Texas Press.

Stanzione, Vincent. 2003. *Rituals of Sacrifice: Walking the Face of the Earth on the Sacred Path of the Sun*. Albuquerque: University of New Mexico Press.

Steggerda, Morris, and Barbara Korsch. 1943. "Remedies for Diseases as Prescribed by Maya Indian Herb-Doctors." *Bulletin of the History of Medicine* 13, no. 1: 54–82.

Stuart, David. 2004. "The Beginnings of the Copan Dynasty: A Review of the Hieroglyphic and Historical Evidence." In *Understanding Early Classic Copan*, edited by Ellen E. Bell, Marcello A. Canuto, and Robert. J. Sharer, 215–48. Philadelphia: University of Pennsylvania Museum of Archaeology and Anthropology.

Stross, Brian. 2007. "The Mesoamerican Sacrum Bone: Doorway to the Otherworld." *FAMSI Journal of the Ancient Americas*. research.famsi.org/aztlan /uploads/papers/stross-sacrum.pdf (accessed 26 October 2015).

Tedlock, Dennis. 1985. *Popol Vuh: The Definitive Edition of the Mayan Book of the Dawn of Life and the Glories of Gods and Kings*. New York: Simon and Schuster.

Tedlock, Dennis. 2003. *Rabinal Achi: A Mayan Drama of War and Sacrifice*. New York: Oxford University Press.

Tiesler, Vera, and Andrea Cucina. 2010. "K'inich Janaab' Pakal se vuelve ancestro. Muerte, sepultura y conmemoración del gobernante palencano." In *Misterios de un rostro maya: La máscara funeraria de K'inich Janaab' Pakal de Palenque*, edited by Laura Filloy Nadal, 91–97. Mexico City: Instituto Nacional de Antropología e Historia.

Tozzer, Alfred M. (1941) 1966. *Landa's Relación de las cosas de Yucatan, A Translation*. Kraus repr. ed. Cambridge, MA: Peabody Museum of American Archaeology and Ethnology, Harvard University.

Villacorta C., J. Antonio, and Flavio Rodas N. 1927. *Manuscrito de Chichicastenango (Popol Buj)*. Guatemala City: Tipografía Sánchez and De Guise.

Vogt, Evon Z. 1976. *Tortillas for the Gods: A Symbolic Analysis of Zinacanteco Rituals*. Cambridge, MA: Harvard University Press.

von Winning, Hasso. 1959. "A Decorated Bone Rattle from Culhuacan, Mexico." *American Antiquity* 25, no. 1: 86–93.

Webster, David. 1997. "Studying Maya Burials." In *Bones of the Maya: Studies of Ancient Skeletons*, edited by Stephen L. Whittington and David M. Reed, 3–12. Washington, DC: Smithsonian Institution Press.

Welsh, W. B. M. 1988. *An Analysis of Classic Lowland Maya Burials*. Oxford, UK: BAR International Series 409.

# The Serpent Within: Birth Rituals and Midwifery Practices in Pre-Hispanic and Colonial Mesoamerican Cultures

Gabrielle Vail, *University of North Carolina at Chapel Hill*

**Abstract.** This article focuses on female-gendered activities in Mesoamerican culture and reveals a strong link between conception, pregnancy, and childbirth on the one hand and weaving and other activities that produce cloth on the other. Supporting evidence from sources such as codices painted during the Postclassic period (13th to 15th centuries) in the northern Maya area indicates that these associations have a longtime depth, spanning at least a millennium. Ethnohistoric sources from highland Guatemala, paired with contemporary practices in that region, provide further insights into beliefs and rituals associated with childbirth and midwifery among prehispanic Maya populations. A review of colonial-period Nahuatl sources provides a comparative perspective for framing the Maya data within the broader context of pre-Conquest Mesoamerica.

Despite the events that have transpired during the past five hundred years in this region, this study finds that many of the elements that were key to this conceptual framework during the Pre-Hispanic period continue to be important today, although their range is more restricted now than it was during the Postclassic and colonial periods. Striking commonalities, as noted, are those that link weaving activities with pregnancy and childbirth. Additionally, objects and iconography related to women and birth—in the form of serpents, umbilical cords, and ropes—tie the act of birth to primordial creation events and highlight the association between midwife and creator grandmother.

**Keywords.** Mexico, Yucatec Maya, Tz'utujiil Maya, Maya codices, midwifery, childbirth, weaving

*Ethnohistory* 66:4 (October 2019)   DOI 10.1215/00141801-7683294

For cultures throughout Mesoamerica, conception, pregnancy, and child-birth are inextricably linked with the activities that contribute to the making of cloth, which include spinning, preparing the threads for the loom (warping), and weaving on the backstrap loom. These conceptual ties span at least a millennium, as suggested by a recent analysis of almanacs from the Postclassic Maya codices, and are of special significance to the Tz'utujiil Maya living today in Santiago Atitlán, Guatemala.

Beliefs and rituals associated with childbirth and midwifery practices among the Maya of highland Guatemala during the colonial period and into the present offer insight into beliefs and practices prior to the Spanish conquest. These beliefs and practices are reflected in painted Maya sources including Postclassic screenfold books and Classic-period pictorial ceramic vessels. When supplemented with material from colonial sources, it becomes possible to model Postclassic Maya healing and midwifery practices associated with childbirth, as well as pre- and postnatal care.

My discussion starts in the ethnographic present, focused on areas with an especially rich tradition of indigenous midwifery practices — including Tz'utujiil Maya groups in the Lake Atitlán region of high-land Guatemala, as well as communities of Yucatec Maya speakers in the northern lowlands of Yucatán — and moves to colonial period practices documented in the same regions (and also in highland Central Mexico, for comparative purposes), and ultimately to pre-Hispanic Yucatec sources that highlight birthing traditions and the activities of midwives.

My methodology relies on the practice of "upstreaming" followed by a number of anthropologists engaged in ethnohistoric research; in other words, I move from "the cultural knowns of the present to the unknown past" (Fenton 1957: 21–22, 1966: 75). In this case, a particular pattern (the metaphorical connections between weaving and childbirth) was identified in contemporary Maya cultures, complementing that previously noted for colonial-period Mesoamerica. The rich Tz'utujiil data led me to re-examine pre-Hispanic Maya written sources (codices) to see if similar patterns could be discerned there. My familiarity with the manuscripts led me to suspect that there would be significant similarities that would serve to validate the methodology, but I also expected to encounter differences as well as a result of both temporal and cultural/geographic distance. As the discussion that follows reveals, both of these expectations were met.

The data are organized geographically as well as temporally. The discussion begins with the present-day highland Maya Tz'utujiil culture and continues with colonial-period sources pertaining to highland Guate-mala and Central Mexico. From there, Yucatec Maya cultures (again mov-ing from the present to the past) become the focus of the discussion.

## Tz'utujiil Midwifery Practices and Associated Deities in the Ethnographic Present

Among the Tz'utujiil and other Maya cultures from highland Guatemala, midwives are classified with herbalists and others who heal with their hands. They may be distinguished in this way from those who rely on supernatural power to bring about cures. The role of midwives in Maya communities today bears a number of similarities to tasks performed by their counterparts during the pre-Hispanic period—that is, examining the pregnant woman during the final months of her pregnancy, prescribing and assisting with steam baths, performing massages and turning the baby if in a breech position, and attending the expectant mother during birth (Villacorta Cifuentes 1976: 139).

In certain areas of highland Guatemala, the womb of a woman is thought to be a coiled snake. If a woman experiences problems before or during delivery, it is believed that the snake is not positioned correctly. Midwives use female head ribbons, similar to those on the cloth bundle representing the creator grandmother Yaxper in the cofradía of San Juan—said to be the womb from which all of humanity derives—to ensure the correct positioning of the serpent womb. Additionally, midwives have a vast repertoire of knowledge of herbal remedies for sterility, menstrual pains, difficult births, and other conditions related to women's health (Orellana 1987). This is supplemented by a reliance on supernatural patrons, a tradition that has its roots in the pre-Hispanic period.

For the Maya of Santiago Atitlán, the deity Yaxper is the patron of midwives.[1] She wears a wrapped cloth headband said to be a serpent, which links her to the sky (the words for "sky" and "serpent" are homophonous in most of the Mayan languages). It may also serve as a marker of the female gender, as male deities almost never appear with serpents as costume elements. Allen Christenson (2001: 95) notes that the serpent headdress worn by Tz'utujiil women is an umbilical cord that connects the wearer to the celestial realm, and more specifically indicates her connection to the moon. In pre-Hispanic contexts (see below), serpents are more commonly associated with the underworld or serve as conduits between the earth's interior and its surface (Miller and Taube 1993: 150; Stone 1995: 23).

Yaxper is envisioned as an elderly female. This fits well with the fact that the role of midwife is taken on by postmenopausal women among the Tz'utujiil, a pattern common throughout the Maya area, not only today but also in the pre-Hispanic past (Cosminsky 2001; Orellana 1987: 66; Sánchez de Aguilar [1639] in Saville 1921: 205; Wisdom 1940: 343, 354). In one of her aspects, Yaxper represents Grandmother Moon (Iyom Pak'lom), an elderly woman with flowing white hair, said to be "secure in knowledge, craft, childbearing, and residence" (Tarn and Prechtel 1986: 174). She may be distinguished in this way from younger women, who are not seen as secure in their domestic role until they are past the age of childbirth. The moon is believed to be the giver of life par excellence and has associations with fertility, conception, and childbirth. According to Nathaniel Tarn and Martin Prechtel's (1986: 174) informant Cristobal Y., "She brought out everything from her belly. She gets big and gives birth to the months. Each month is born out of her: these are the twelve Marías."

The twelve Marías are linked to the twelve Martíns, gods who represent the female and male principles, respectively. (The thirteenth member of each set is considered anomalous and separate from the other twelve.) In her role as midwife (*iyom*), Yaxper is also called María Isabela. She plays an important role in Tz'utujiil conceptions of birth, as do several of the other Marías, including the lake (María) as the womb, (María) Concepción as the one who gives birth, and (María) Rosario as the earthly mother of Jesús (Tarn and Prechtel 1986: 180).

Within Santiago Atitlán, the confraternity (or cofradía) of San Juan contains a cloth bundle representing Yaxper, housed in a box suspended from the ceiling (Christenson 2001: 122). The bundle has ribbons attached to it that are symbolic of umbilical cords and the tendrils of plants. It has the faces of three of the Marías, known as the "three corn girls," who are named María (Yamri), Concepción (Yachon), and Juana (Yaxuan). It is used in rituals during pregnancy and in healing ceremonies for sick infants. During the former, it is placed face down on the abdomen of the pregnant woman; whichever of the three Marías is nearest her navel will give the child its "face," or character. At the base of the bundle are two round, hard cloth bags said to contain the original seeds, or placentas, of the human race, in the form of divine twins (one male and one female); they are called "the root of children," "the first midwives," and "the first birthmakers." The bundle itself is believed to be the primordial womb from which all of humanity is descended. The box containing the bundle hangs from the ceiling to show its link to the moon, which serves as the patron of midwives (Tarn and Prechtel 1986: 175–76). The midwife takes the expectant mother to the confraternity house during her seventh or eighth month of pregnancy on the night of a full moon so that she can bathe in the moon's light. The midwife also places a bowl of water in front of her so that she can speak to the moon's reflection (Christenson 2001: 121).

During an earlier era, the twelve Marías created a deity called the Mam from the wood of the *tzite'* tree (Erythrina) in order to control the forces of chaos in the world. However, rather than reflecting the principles of order, his mischief making and hypersexuality led to greater chaos. The Marías therefore disassembled his body, which is only reassembled (by members of the cofradía of Santa Cruz) when he is needed. The Mam is the thirteenth Martín and has two wives. The younger of the two wives, María Castellana, is closer in age to a daughter and is associated with songs, flowers, and a proclivity toward wantonness. His older wife is the thirteenth María, known as Francisca Batz'bal ("Thread Maker"), who is described as an older woman, past menopause, who is a sorceress (Tarn and Prechtel 1986: 178).

An image of Francisca Batz'bal is kept in the cofradía house of the Mam, where it is wrapped in a scarf so that only the head and face show. The body is said to be a weaving stand, representing the original María—an old lady who uses a batten to comb her hair, which produces corn cobs. She and the other Marías are believed to have woven their children (birds, jaguars, snakes, and so forth) into the mantle of the earth. Metaphorically, cloth and children are linked, and the twelve Marías are understood to be parts of the loom and also signify the first twelve months of a child's life (Tarn and Prechtel 1986: 176).

Woven cloth is conceptualized as representing a year, as it moves ever closer to the post to which the loom is tied (believed to represent the world tree).[2] The rope that connects the loom to the post or tree is called an umbilical cord, and one of the epithets for the Mam (su'tin ala) refers to him as a weaving stand full of cloth. The Mam's María (Francisca Batz'bal) is associated with the batten, the shed stick, and the heddle, whereas the other loom parts are aspects of the other Marías. These deified loom components—together referred to as the Ixoc Ahaua—are used by the midwife during prenatal care and delivery (Tarn and Pretchel 1986: 176). For example, in turning a breech infant, the midwife first places the appropriate loom component on the abdomen of the expectant mother, which is meant to coax the infant to turn. Following this, the midwife physically turns the infant, an action that would not be attempted without first invoking the aid of the Ixoc Ahaua through the loom part.[3] Weaving implements are also used by the midwife—who becomes Grandmother Moon (Iyom Pak'lom, or Yaxper) while assisting with labor—to call on the Ixoc Ahaua to produce birthing contractions. The deified loom elements are also helpful for treating menstrual problems (Prechtel and Carlsen 1988: 124).

Weaving and birth are further connected by the way that the board used for preparing the threads for the loom (the warping board) and the loom itself are conceptualized as being human in form, in terms of having a head, heart, and other body parts (see Prechtel and Carlsen 1988: 125). Moreover, the phrases used to describe the completion of a textile and the birth of a child include "The weaving is born," and "The child is woven [into existence]." Scholars have suggested that these associations may relate to the sexual connotations associated with the act of spinning thread (the penetration of the spindle whorl by the spindle) and the resemblance of a spindle thickening with thread to the fetus growing in the womb (Sullivan 1982: 14; see also discussion in the section on Central Mexico below).

The designation of the Mam's María as Francisca Batz'bal identifies her both as the thread maker and as the spindle (*batz'*). The thread that she spins is the Mam himself. He, in turn, uses a variety of means (including thread and rope, as well as poison and drugs) to entrap humans by means of witchcraft. Francisca Batz'bal likewise has associations with sorcery; she is said to use her spindle to drill holes into muscles and bone and to be the cause of epilepsy. Moreover, the box in which the Mam's clothes are stored in the cofradía house is said to be full of pain and sickness (Tarn and Prechtel 1986: 177), suggesting that he also causes illness. Indeed, he is associated with a number of childhood diseases (184n17). Despite this, the Mam plays a role as the guardian of children and is called on by the midwife, who burns incense and candles to call him to be present during childbirth. How difficult the birth is depends on how pleased the Mam is by the offerings that have been provided. The point at which he "enters his road" is believed to be what causes the woman's cervix to open during a birth.

Also present when a woman gives birth are the Ixok Ahaua (female guardians), aspects of the twelve Marías. Rather than serving as protectors, however, they play a role similar to the *tzitzimime* of Nahuatl mythology who threaten women during childbirth. It is said, for example, that if the candles set out to burn for them go out, the child will die. Similarly, the mother's life may be forfeited if she does not follow the correct prohibitions associated with childbirth (179).

Following birth, the midwife continues to play a crucial role, by binding the child with its father's belt to keep it safe and warm, and giving the mother a steam bath or a chocolate drink to replenish the heat loss caused by birth (179, 184n17).[4] After the child is delivered, the midwife brings its placenta to the cofradía house to be blessed, after which time it is wrapped in cloth and buried near the family's hearth or thrown into the lake, where it resides with the lake aspect of María (Mendelson 1957: 227, 548n11, cited in Christenson 2001: 122).

### Midwifery Practices in Highland Guatemala during the Colonial Period

Seventeenth-century reports from highland Guatemala suggest that childbirth took place in the steam bath rather than in the house (a practice also followed by the Aztec for difficult births). Husbands were present to assist the midwife; among the Pipil, both would let blood to petition the deities when the birth was not progressing as it should (García de Palacio 1927: 76, 88). Herbal remedies were also frequently used, including *cihuapahtli* (Montanoa tomentosa Cerv.), the root of which was used to make a drink to induce contractions. Today, the whole plant is used to make a tea that causes uterine contractions during birth (Mellen 1974: 149), a remedy also mentioned by Francisco de Fuentes y Guzmán (1969–72 1:241) for seventeenth-century Guatemala.

Each of the objects used on the day of a child's birth was afterward offered to a spring or river, and a divination was performed to determine when the umbilical cord should be cut (Las Casas 1967 2:227–28). This was done over an ear of maize, from which the kernels were removed and planted. Once the maize was harvested, a gruel was made for the child, and some kernels were kept for male children to plant as adults. The rest of the harvest went to the priest or diviner.

Fuentes y Guzmán (1969–72 1:280–81) describes a similar ritual in which blood from the umbilical cords of boys was burned while an ear of maize was passed through its smoke; afterward, the maize seeds were planted in the family's milpa, and the child was fed from the maize grown from these seeds until he was old enough to plant for himself. Although neither source mentions a midwife being involved in these ceremonies, she is likely the one who cut the child's umbilical cord, as is the custom in the Maya highlands today as well as in colonial-period Central Mexico (see below).

Evidence from colonial sources suggests that sweat baths played an important role in birth rituals in colonial Maya culture (and in all likelihood significantly further back in time), as was also the case among the Aztec. Steam baths had their own deity patrons, including Francisca Batz'bal and the Mam for the Tz'utujiil Maya and paired male-female earth lords for highland Chiapas (Groark 1997). According to ethnographic sources, Maya midwives often buried the afterbirth, either in the sweat bath (Wagley 1949: 23) or in the hearth of an abandoned home (Taube 1994: 668).

## Midwifery Practices and Associated Deities in Colonial-Period Central Mexico

Spanish colonial sources provide only scant documentation pertaining to midwives and childbirth practices for the lowland Maya region, although Timothy Knowlton and Edber Dzidz Yam (this issue) discuss the rich material relating to perinatal rites found in indigenous Yucatec-language documents from this time period (discussed below). Comparative material is largely to be found in sources pertaining to highland central Mexico, where this topic receives extensive coverage in Bernandino de Sahagún's *Florentine Codex*, or *Historia general de las cosas de Nueva España*. This 2,400-page ethnography, completed in 1569, was compiled, illustrated, and written (in Nahuatl and Spanish) by a group of former Nahua students of Sahagún's under the friar's oversight. Book 6, "Rhetoric and Moral Philosophy," devotes fifteen chapters to the conduct expected of pregnant women, their families, and the midwives hired to care for them. A brief discussion of this material is included below, as it speaks to the central focus of this essay on beliefs and practices crosscutting the female sphere of childbirth, spinning, and weaving and helps to inform our understanding of Maya practices from the same time period. A number of the themes presented in the previous section thread through the discussion, including the link between childbirth and the production of cloth; ties between pregnant women, midwives, and the moon; and conceptual links among steam baths, earth deities, and symbolic wombs.

### Deity Patrons of Midwives in Colonial Sources

Among the Nahuatl cultures of highland central Mexico, a complex of deities can be recognized as having links to midwives and their ritual and healing practices, Tlazolteotl-Ixcuina being foremost among them (Sullivan 1982). As Thelma D. Sullivan (1982) notes, Tlazolteotl-Ixcuina — originally the mother goddess of the Huastec culture — came to play a significant role among the Mexica culture as the goddess of medicine and medicinal plants, and as the patron of healers and midwives, in addition to her other roles (see Knowlton 2016 and Sullivan 1982). She was also known to "those who provide the herbs for aborting" (Sahagún 1950–82 1:47) and had a special relationship to cotton, which was used both for weaving and for medicine.[5] Her costume identifies her with spinners, specifically the use of unspun cotton and spindle whorls worn in the hair (Sullivan 1982: 8). These costume elements also symbolize her link to conception, pregnancy, and birth. As Sullivan (1982: 14) notes, "The spindle set in the spindle whorl is symbolic of coitus, and the thread, as it winds around the spindle, symbolizes the growing fetus." Weaving is likewise thought to be symbolic of the sexual act, suggesting that the activities associated with weaving (spinning, warping, etc.) can be viewed as representing the life cycle (14).

Tlazolteotl-Ixcuina's close association with cotton may relate to her role as a healer as well as a weaver. Sullivan (1982: 19) notes that the bark of the cotton plant was efficacious for inducing labor (i.e., for bringing on uterine contractions) and menstruation, whereas an extract of the pulverized seeds was administered to aid lactation. These uses have been documented in both central Mexico and Yucatán (Hernández 1959 1:426; Martínez 1944: n.p.; Ossado 1834: 21, 25; cited in Sullivan 1982: 19). In light of her role as a healer, Tlazolteotl-Ixcuina's lunar associations are of particular interest.

The youthful deity Xochiquetzal, identified by Diego Durán (1971: 239) as the patron of craftspeople, has also been associated with the moon (Nicholson 1971: 421; Klein 1975: 73; Seler 1960–61 5:188, cited in Milbrath 1995: 57). She is commonly shown with a weaving batten and is identified as the inventor of weaving and embroidery in the *Codex Ríos* (Corona Núñez 1964–67). Like María Castellana in Santiago Atitlán today, she is said to have many different sexual partners (Durán 1971: 68), a common characteristic of the moon goddess in ethnographic accounts (Báez-Jorge 1983: 402, 404; Ichon 1973: 65; Thompson 1939: 135–36).

Mayahuel, the goddess of maguey, was also associated with spinning and weaving among central Mexican cultures. She is described as "the embodiment of female productivity and reproductivity" (Sullivan 1982: 25) and may be linked to weaving, medicine, and healing. Like cotton, the maguey plant had important medicinal uses, one of which was to induce menstruation (Sahagún 1950–82 11:217; Hernández 1959 1:348–52). Additionally, it was used to cleanse the kidneys and bladder and to dissolve gallstones (Sahagún 1950–82 11:217; Hernández 1959 1:348–52).

Another deity of interest, Cihuacoatl, or "Serpent Woman" (Sahagún 1950–82, 7:160; Torquemada 1943 1:81), plays an important role in the festival of Tititl, where she holds a batten, suggesting that she embodies both a weaving goddess and a female warrior (Milbrath 1995: 68).[6] Cecelia Klein (1982: 1) points out that *tititl* means "stretching" and suggests that this may refer to stretching the threads on a warping frame, an activity depicted in the *Madrid Codex* (see discussion below). This fits well with Sahagún's (1950–82 1: 15, 6:160) identification of Cihuacoatl as a patron of midwives.

The age-based dichotomies that characterize the central Mexican deities referenced above recall the Tz'utujiil María complex with its arrangement of linked deities who each have different associations and aspects. One of the aspects of Tlazolteotl-Ixcuina was Temazcalteci, "Grandmother of the Bathhouse" (Sullivan 1982: 17–18). This deity is of particular relevance to our discussion, given her importance to pregnant women and newly delivered mothers, who undertook steam baths according to a regimen developed by their midwife (Sahagún 1950–82, 11:191; Durán 1971: 269–72) (fig. 1). Sullivan (1982: 18), noting that the hearth of a steam bath is called *xictli*, which also means "navel," equates the steam bath structure with the warm,

Figure 1. **Woman tending a steam bath on** *Codex Tudela*, **62r, courtesy of the Museo de América, Madrid.**

moist womb of the mother goddess, much as it is conceptualized by the Maya of Santiago Atitlán today.

### Colonial Birthing Practices

The *Florentine Codex* tells us that the midwife was called four or five days before an Aztec woman gave birth. When the birth was imminent, the midwife accompanied her to the steam bath, where she was bathed and given a drink made from the root of an herb called *cihuapahtli* (Montanoa tomentosa Cerv.), mentioned previously in relation to the Maya highlands, to induce contractions. This was sometimes followed by a small dosage of ground-up opossum tail (considered to be a powerful expellant), if her labor was difficult. If labor continued for longer than a day and night, another sweat bath was administered, and prayers were offered to the appropriate deities (Sahagún 1950–82, 7:159–60).

Following childbirth, the midwife might administer a sweat bath to purify the new mother. The *Códice Carolina* (Garibay 1967: 57) describes a ritual occurring at this time, during which the new mother tossed cotton into the hearth or navel (*xictli*) of the bathhouse. This was intended as an offering to the womb of the mother goddess, who symbolized the earth (Sullivan 1982: 18).

The midwife was responsible for giving the newborn its first bath, which was dedicated to the goddess of water Chalchiuhtlicue (Sahagún 1950–82, 7:176). After a period of celebration, the parents summoned the soothsayer to determine the child's fate based on the day on which it was born (Sahagún 1950–82, 7:159–60). This was followed by a second bathing ceremony administered by the midwife, who introduced the child to the items made for him or her—a little shield, bow, and arrows for boys, and a spindle whorl, batten, reed basket, spinning bowl, cotton skeins, and shuttle for girls.[7] A similar ritual, called the *hedzmek* (spelled *héetz méek'* in the orthography used for written Yucatec today), is practiced in the Maya area (Duncan and Hofling 2011; Redfield and Villa Rojas 1934: 182). At the age of three or four months, babies are first carried astride the hip by the godparent of the same sex, who also introduces the child to different objects that it will use in adulthood, according to its gender (i.e., a machete for a boy, or a grinding stone for a girl).

## Midwifery Practices in Contemporary Yucatán

As is the case in much of Mesoamerica, pregnant women in Yucatán also receive massages throughout pregnancy. Just prior to childbirth, a final massage is performed to make sure the uterus and the baby are both in the correct position (Redfield and Villa Rojas 1934: 360). Unlike the practice seen in Santiago Atitlán, however, there is no indication that weaving implements are involved in this manipulation. Moreover, in at least certain contemporary communities, a male healer, or *h-meen*, assists with difficult births, rather than a woman playing this role. One particularly interesting fact noted by Knowlton and Dzidz Yam (this issue) from the interviews is that some Yucatec healers report passing a cotton ball composed of thirteen threads over a pregnant woman who is experiencing a difficult childbirth. This is one of the few associations still seen of what was once a vibrant tradition in which pregnancy, childbirth, and making cloth were intimately linked.

Following the birth, the midwife traditionally used a reed to cut the umbilical cord (Redfield and Villa Rojas 1934: 182) and made sure that the newborn and mother were kept warm. This involved being placed near a fire and/or being given foods or drinks associated with heat in the Maya ethnophysiological classificatory system. One of these described by Robert Redfield and Alfonso Villa Rojas (1934: 183) was a hot chocolate beverage sweetened with honey. We know that a similar beverage was prepared during the Late Classic period (600–900 CE), but there is nothing to indicate that it was meant for a woman following pregnancy.

According to ethnographic sources, Yucatec midwives either burned the afterbirth or buried it in the hearth of an abandoned home (182). This is similar to the practice in the highland region of burying it in the sweat bath. Although little evidence exists today of this practice in the Maya lowlands, colonial sources suggest that sweat baths played an important role in birth rituals in colonial Maya culture (and in all likelihood significantly further back in time). Knowlton and Dzidz Yam (this issue) provide compelling evidence that this was the case in Yucatán as well as in other parts of the Maya area.

## Midwifery Practices in Colonial Yucatán

### Colonial Spanish Sources

Colonial-period sources relating to the northern Maya lowlands include only occasional mentions of female deities, although they provide other important details about daily and ritual life. The best known of these sources is the *Relación de las cosas de Yucatán*, which was compiled by Diego de Landa, a Franciscan friar (and later a bishop) who served in Yucatán for much of his adult life after arriving in 1549. Landa's discussion of female deities centers on Ix Chel, who is described as the patron of childbirth and midwives and also is a goddess of medicine and divination (Tozzer 1941: 10n45, 154). Landa notes that women of childbearing age placed images of this deity under their beds and sought her assistance and guidance (129), and that pilgrimages were made to her shrine on the island of Cozumel by those wishing to petition her for special favors. Other pilgrimage shrines associated with female deities were those to Ix Chekel (also spelled Chebel) Yax, Ix Hunie, and Ix Hunieta on Isla Mujeres (9–10). Of those cited in colonial sources, only Ix Chel (also sometimes called Chak Chel) appears in earlier pre-Hispanic sources (discussed in the section on pre-Hispanic midwifery practices below). Diego López de Cogolludo ([1688] 1955 Bk. 4: chap. 8) describes Ix Chekel Yax as the daughter of the sun and the patron of brocading. Her mother, Ix Azal Uoh (also spelled Ix Asal Woh), is said to be the wife of the sun and the inventor of weaving (Bk. 4: chap. 8).[8]

In colonial-period Yucatec sources, Ix Chel, as the goddess of medicine, is invoked in the ceremony called Ihcil-Ixchel ("the bath of Ix Chel") celebrated by the "physicians and sorcerers" and their wives during the month of Sip.[9] The name of the ceremony derives from the fact that the physicians and sorcerers were said to have carried bundles containing small "idols" of Ix Chel, as well as divining stones. Landa (in Tozzer 1941: 129) reports that the "sorceresses" (midwives) placed an image of Ix Chel near their patient during childbirth, a practice that recalls visiting the Tz'utujiil image of Francisca Batz'bal that is in the cofradía house of Santa Cruz.

Pedro Sánchez de Aguilar ([1639] 1921: 205) also notes the importance of midwives (whom he calls "old Indian shamans"), who hear the confessions of pregnant women, a practice also common among the Aztec. In sixteenth-century idolatry trials, midwives were described as sorceresses or enchantresses (*viejas hechiceras*) and were mentioned along with other ritual practitioners, including the *ah kin* ("diviners") and *chilan* ("prophets") (Scholes and Adams 1938: 133, cited in Tozzer 1941: 129n598). Their role included attending women prior to and during birth, likely in a manner similar to that described for Yucatec cultures in the ethnographic present. Following birth, the child was immediately bathed by the midwife; later, the newborn would be taken to the priest, who determined their fate and eventual profession, and gave them their childhood name (Tozzer 1941: 129). Parallels with Aztec practices are readily apparent.

A "rebirth" ritual is also known for colonial Yucatán, called *caput sihil*, which Landa translates as "to be born anew" (see Tozzer 1941: 102). This occurs long after birth, however, and appears to be a coming-of-age ceremony, in which "an old woman for the girls and a man for the boys" served as godparents (103), the former likely being a midwife.[10]

*Indigenous Sources*

Knowlton and Dzidz Yam's analysis (this issue) of perinatal chants from the *Ritual of the Bacabs* reveals a wealth of linkages between the conceptual domains of pregnancy and birth, on the one hand, and textile production and weaving, on the other. For example, they note that the warping frame (*chuch*) is referenced in one of the chants in the Ritual of the Bacabs, and that a deity paired with Chacal Ix Chel (an aspect of the creator goddess) is said to be the icon of the warping frame. This is of interest given the important role warping frames play in the almanacs connecting weaving and birth in the *Madrid Codex* (see discussion below).

Other terms from the chants pertaining to perinatal practices discussed by Knowlton and Dzidz Yam that are polysemous include *ibin*, which is used to mean "placenta," although the authors note that it is more commonly applied to "thread" or "net"; and *ḱilil*, which refers to both something unwoven and to a woman who is not a virgin. The former definition recalls several almanacs in the *Dresden Codex* that will be discussed in a subsequent section. Other phrases that are relevant to the pre-Hispanic materials include *kamex chab* (*k'amex ch'ab'* in the orthography I use for the codices), which Knowlton and Dzidz Yam (this issue) translate as "receive the infant," and *x alansah* "she who facilitates birth." Similar phrases occur in the almanac on page 2d of the *Dresden Codex*, which I analyze below.

A final chant of interest to our discussion includes that for expelling the afterbirth. Knowlton and Dzidz Yam (this issue) note that the deity patron who is named is related to the *balche'* tree, the bark of which is used to make an alcoholic drink that was commonly served at feasts. One interpretation of her patronage in this particular context is that balche' was efficacious in expelling the afterbirth. In addition to being used to make an intoxicating beverage, sources indicate that the maguey plant was used medicinally by the Aztec. Perhaps this was true of the balche' tree as well.

### Pre-Hispanic Maya Midwifery Practices

Pre-Hispanic and colonial sources from the lowland Maya area point to the fact that midwives were most commonly postmenopausal women, as is also true for the Tz'utujiil Maya today. Their deity patron was named Ix ("Lady") or Chak ("Red, Great") Chel.[11] This deity-as-midwife presided over childbirth practices, such as those depicted on the "Birth Vase" (discussed below). Images of Chak Chel clearly depict her as an elderly figure wearing the accoutrements associated with midwives, including a headdress consisting of a serpent (or a twisted cloth symbolic serpent) and, at times, spindles wound with cotton thread. As Mary Ciaramella (1994) notes, both headdress types identify the wearers as having commonalities with the grandmother deity of weaving, conception, and childbirth among the Tz'utujiil. Her serpent associations, however, suggest a link to the watery realm within the earth, rather than to the sky. In pre-Hispanic contexts, serpents are often portrayed as conduits between the underworld and the earth, as is discussed in more detail below.

Chak Chel is occasionally depicted weaving or sewing in the Maya codices, but more commonly she gives birth to the rains (often paired with the rain deity Chaak), in either their life-giving or destructive form.[12] She and Chaak also appear together in several murals from Postclassic contexts at the Caribbean site of Tulum, where they are associated with the fertile underworld realm and are depicted as creating humans from ground maize seed (Vail and Hernández 2012).

During the pre-Hispanic period, Chak Chel only appears explicitly as a midwife on one occasion—a pottery vessel that has been nicknamed the "Birth Vase" (Taube 1994). While its exact provenience remains unknown, studies conducted by Dorie Reents-Budet (personal communication to

Taube 1993; cited in Taube 1994: 653) suggest that it falls within the canons of Late Classic pottery traditions of the central Petén area of present-day Guatemala. Chak Chel appears multiple times on this four-sided vessel, which researchers suggest may have been intended to represent a house. On one of its sides, she is shown assisting with a delivery in the home of the woman (or goddess) giving birth, who grasps twisted cords suspended from the ceiling (Taube 1994: 658). These cords are reminiscent of those used by the Tz'utujiil to suspend the María cloth from the ceiling of the cofradía house to express a link with the sky realm.[13] Karl A. Taube (1994: 659) notes that similar birthing cords are still used in some Mesoamerican communities today.

The woman preparing to give birth and the midwife behind her stand on what has been identified as a personified *witz*, or mountain (661). This draws attention to Chak Chel's association with the earth's interior, which may be entered through caves within mountains, as well as sweat baths, seen as symbolic caves (Moyes 2005). The underworld, or realm within the earth, is a place of fertility and conception among Mesoamerican cultures (Prechtel and Carlsen 1988; Tarn and Prechtel 1986). For the contemporary Tz'utujiil, it is the realm of females, the home of the moon, and the birthplace of celestial beings (Prechtel and Carlsen 1988: 126–217). The entrance to this realm is said to be guarded by a giant serpent, and the sinuous passages of caves have also been described as serpentlike in nature (Christenson 2001).

Chak Chel appears in the role of midwife three separate times on the following side of the vessel. In two cases, she holds bowls of water, which Taube (1994: 664) suggests were used to bathe the infant just after birth, similar to the ritual described in the *Florentine Codex* and by Landa for the Yucatec Maya. The third Chak Chel is standing and reaches toward an open-mouthed serpent, from which a child-sized Pawahtun emerges (Taube 1994: 664), a convention commonly used to depict birth, presumably from the underworld realm. Taube (1994: 664), noting a connection between the Pre-Hispanic Pawahtun deities and the Mam that plays such an important role in highland Guatemala, interprets this scene in light of contemporary Tz'utujiil birth rituals in which the midwife invites the Mam to be present at the birth and suggests that this represents the assigning of the infant's *way*, or animal alter ego. Alternatively, it may symbolize the calling of the Mam into being for the first time, an act performed by the aged creator goddess Francisca Batz'bal among the Tz'utujiil (Tarn and Prechtel 1986: 177), and, by extension, possibly also by Chak Chel for the lowland Maya. The presence of the quadripartite Pawahtun figures (thought to be related to the Mam) seated amid the sky "umbilicus" on page 22 of the *Paris Codex* (fig. 2) calls this act to mind, especially as it occurs amid scenes of death

Figure 2.   Pawahtun deities seated on skyband and surrounded by an "umbilicus" on page 22 of the *Paris Codex* (*Codex Peresianus*) (Rosny 1888: Pl. 22), courtesy of Boundary End Center, Barnardsville, NC.

Figure 3. Couples facing each other in the almanac on pages 93b–94b of the *Madrid Codex* (*Troano Codex*) (Brasseur de Bourbourg 1869–70: Plates XIX-XX). Several, if not all, of the females appear to be pregnant. Courtesy of Boundary End Center, Barnardsville, NC.

deities being conjured or "born" from the gaping mouths of serpents at the bottom of the page.

Moreover, carved representations of Chak Chel at Chichén Itzá paired with Pawahtuns provide additional support for the paired role this deity "couple" plays in events associated with creation and primordial time (Stone 1999).

Several almanacs in the Maya codices may depict midwives in the guise of weavers, whereas one almanac from the *Madrid Codex* shows examples of pregnant women (or possibly female deities), seated facing male deity partners (fig. 3).

An elderly female deity who can be distinguished from Chak Chel (discussed below) occurs on several occasions in almanacs related to the care of the stingless bees and the harvest of their honey. It has been suggested that she may be a midwife (Vail and Stone 2002), since honey was used to treat pregnant women. Northeastern Yucatán, where the *Madrid Codex* was likely painted (Chuchiak 2004), was an important honey-producing region at the time (Batún Alpuche et al. 2017). Additionally, in contemporary Yucatec Maya communities such as Oxkutzkab, the word *hobon* refers to both the log in which stingless bees have their hives and to a woman's womb (Hanks 1990; cited in Jong 1999: 306). It has been suggested that the two are connected by the fact that both are conceived of as relating to the earth (Jong 1999: 306).[14]

Figure 4. Female deities, likely Chak Chel, are shown producing water from their bodies on pages 30b and 32b of the *Madrid Codex* (*Troano Codex*) (Brasseur de Bourbourg 1869–70: Plates XXV, XXVII), courtesy of Boundary End Center, Barnardsville, NC.

Figure 5.    The goddess Chalchiuhlicue on *Codex Borgia* 65 (after Kingsborough 1830–48). © The Trustees of the British Museum. All rights reserved.

Childbirth per se is not depicted in the Maya codices, although other types of birth—of cloth and of the rains—are. Nevertheless, there are a handful of occasions in which deities are depicted in a posture reminiscent of birth. It is interesting that this posture is most commonly assumed by male deities rather than females; these include Chaak (who gives birth to the rains) and the death god (who typically does not produce water).[15] Although Chak Chel is at times pictured producing rain waters from an overturned vessel, female deities are only associated with the creation of rain/water from their bodies on two occasions (fig. 4).

In both examples, the deities are shown standing (rather than in a squatting position), with fluids emerging not only from the vaginal area, but also from the armpits and/or mouth. The two relevant figures have distended lips and other abnormalities, suggesting that they might represent the rain waters associated with storms.[16] They wear spindles wound with thread as headdress elements, likely congruent with those worn by deities such as Tlazolteotl-Ixcuina, as well as serpents and/or twisted cloth headdresses similar to those worn by Maya women in highland Guatemala, which serve to link them with the grandmother deity of weaving, conception, and childbirth. The waters emitted from their bodies call to mind images of the central Mexican deity Chalchiuhlicue, who is associated with bathing rituals linked to childbirth, as well as to scenes of death and destruction (fig. 5).

Figure 6. Ritual "anointing" of children on pages 92c–93c of the *Madrid Codex* (*Troano Codex*) (Brasseur de Bourbourg 1869–70: Plates XX-XXI), courtesy of Boundary End Center, Barnardsville, NC.

Water imagery is also of central importance in the almanac on page 92c–93c of the *Madrid Codex* (fig. 6), which features a figure who may represent an elderly midwife, who is involved in bathing a second figure (likely intended as a child).[17]

This almanac has a number of correspondences to the "rebirth," or puberty, ceremony described by Landa (Tozzer 1941: 102–06), in which children of both sexes underwent a ritual "cleansing" as part of the process by which they passed out of childhood and were considered ready to assume adult responsibilities. Landa notes that godparents were selected for each group of children, with an elderly female (likely a midwife) being chosen for the girls (103). The almanac's four frames each begin with one of the four world directions (proceeding from east to north to west to south), followed by a compound that refers to a bath (*ichkil*). The names of several deities are also mentioned, including that of the wind and flower deity, who had positive, life-affirming qualities. This recalls the Aztec ceremony in which children received their names based on the day of their birth in the divinatory calendar, and a similar ritual which is alluded to briefly for the Yucatec Maya by Landa (129).

An elderly female similar in appearance to the figure in the second frame of the almanac in question appears in a number of other contexts in the *Madrid Codex*. Of particular interest are those that depict activities associated with the production of cloth. As previously discussed, the Tz'utujiil Maya anthropomorphize both the loom and the board used for warping the thread prior to placing it on the loom. The warping frame, for

Figure 7.    Weaving almanac on page 102b of the *Madrid Codex* (*Troano Codex*) (Brasseur de Bourbourg 1869–70: Pl. XI), courtesy of Boundary End Center, Barnardsville, NC.

example, has a head, foot, and heart, whereas the loom has an umbilicus, through which the weaving receives sustenance. It is tied to the mother tree by a rope called *yujkut*, which signifies "umbilical cord" (Pretchel and Carlsen 1988: 125). Like a child, a weaving is said to be born, or like the sun, to "come out."

These ideas have clear pre-Hispanic antecedents, as suggested by two cognate almanacs in the *Madrid Codex*. The first, on page 102b (fig. 7), pictures two deities weaving—an elderly female in the first frame whose name consists of a *sak* ("white") prefix, followed by a portrait glyph (T1027) that has been variously read as *ix* ("woman") or *kab'* ("earth") (Vail and Stone 2002),[18] and a death or underworld deity in the second.

Both figures are pictured using a backstrap loom to weave cloth; the loom is attached to a tree by a rope, or what the Tz'utujiil identify as an umbilical cord. The association with birth is further highlighted by the verb that begins the two captions (T812), which has a meaning such as "to be born" or "dawn" (note that the glyph shows the sun rising next to a symbol that represents *ak'b'al*, "night" or "darkness"). The birth metaphor is highlighted by the use of the glyph *y-al(en)*, 'her child', at the end of the first clause. The phrase as a whole states: "The goddess' child [i.e., her weaving] dawns/comes out/is born from the tree."

This is paralleled by the almanac found on page 102d of the *Madrid Codex* (fig. 8), which is almost identical iconographically (note that the

Figure 8. Weaving almanac on page 102d of the *Madrid Codex* (*Troano Codex*) (Brasseur de Bourbourg 1869–70: Pl. XI), courtesy of Boundary End Center, Barnardsville, NC.

same two deities are pictured; here, however, the elderly female in the first frame wears a hank of cotton thread in her hair).

Variant name glyphs are used, however, consisting of the deity's portrait glyph (minus *sak* in frame one), followed by a suffix spelling *chel* (*che-le*), which also appears in the name Chak Chel. Moreover, the first glyph in each frame also differs from that in the previous almanac. Instead of T812, the compound consists of *o-chi-ya*, giving *ochiy*, meaning both "to enter" and "food." It is likely that the verb was meant here, giving rise to the phrase "The goddess Ix (Kab') Chel's [weaving] entered from the tree." The latter reading (as "food") is also a possibility, however, as the act of weaving is said to give sustenance to the cloth.

A cognate deity is seen in the first two frames of the almanac on page 102c of the *Madrid Codex*, followed by two frames that name but do not picture deities; these include the death god and the creator Itzamna. This almanac depicts the warping frame (*chuch*), which is mentioned in the chant discussed by Knowlton and Dzidz Yam (this issue), where X Bolon Puc (Lady Nine Hills) is named as its icon. The hieroglyphic caption to the almanac's first frame reads: *sinah u chuch sak kab'/ix oox wi'il*, "White Lady (Earth's) warping frame is stretched, [leading to] an abundance of food." The verb used in this context is semantically equivalent to Tititl, the name of the Aztec festival in which Cihuacoatl ("Serpent Woman") is featured with a weaving batten. While the deity in the *Madrid Codex* is not shown with a serpent, she wears a figure-eight headdress, which is symbolically associated with serpents according to Ciaramella's (1994) analysis.

A similar headdress is worn by the Maya goddess in the first frame of the almanac on page 102d of the *Madrid Codex*, who is named with the *chel* suffix. Its use in this context suggests that the elderly (earth?) deity may be an aspect of the creator goddess Chak Chel. The two are occasionally conflated, as for example on page 2b of the *Dresden Codex* (fig. 9a), where Chak Ix/Kab' Chel and the flower/wind deity appear sewing a textile in the first frame, and the wife of the death god does the same in the following scene. This almanac and the one in the register below both show what may be the *ibin* referenced in one of the chants discussed by Knowlton and Dzidz Yam (this issue), which can have the meaning of "thread" or "net" but also refers to the placenta. In each of the relevant examples, it appears to be the wife of the deity pictured who is performing the activity named *chuy* ("to sew"). The almanac in the bottom register on the same page (fig. 9b) shows a youthful aspect of the elderly (earth?) deity in the first frame, and the death god in the second.

They hold skirts (note that the skirt is folded in the first frame), and the hieroglyphic captions refer to their act of receiving the skirts (*u k'am u pik*, "she received her skirt"). This calls to mind the chant that referred to the infant being received in the Ritual of the Bacabs (Knowlton and Dzidz Yam, this issue), and suggests the same type of metaphorical equivalence of cloth and infants seen in the Tz'utujiil Maya worldview. In this regard, it is of interest that the youthful goddess's name is followed by the same compound *y-al(en)* as that of the elderly deity on page 102b of the *Madrid Codex*. It appears that they are both associated with birth and children (in the form of textiles), or that both figures are being named as midwives (a shortened form of *x alansah*).

The three female deities portrayed in the codices may be different aspects of a single female principle, as is the case for the María complex of the Tz'utujiil Maya. The young deity is shown as a wife/sexual partner, as pregnant, and with a child. She also carries omens and burdens that serve as prognostications for different time periods, and exchanges honeycomb (used to sweeten the chocolate drink served during marriage negotiations and to mothers following childbirth) with the creator Itzamna.[19] The elderly counterpart of this figure is shown performing a bathing ceremony, stretching her warping frame, weaving, and in almanacs associated with the care of the stingless bees and the extraction of honey from their hives.[20] All of these are activities attributed to midwives in the ethnographic and ethnohistoric literature.

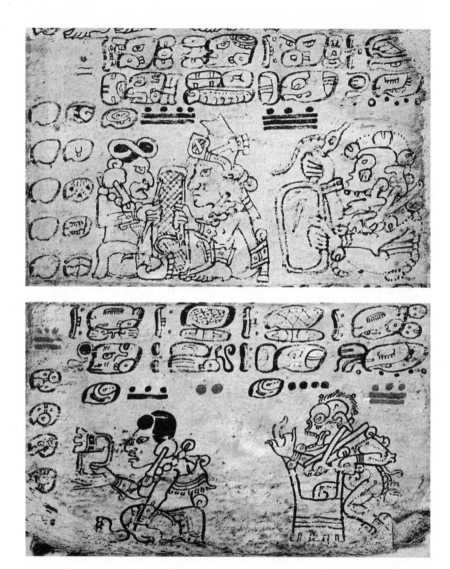

Figures 9a (top) and b (bottom).   Scenes associated with the creation of textiles on page 2b and 2d of the *Dresden Codex* (after Förstemann 1880), courtesy of Boundary End Center, Barnardsville, NC.

In the examples in which Sak Ix/Kab' appears in the beekeeping section, she wears hanks of cotton in her hair. As previously noted, cotton plays an important role in birth rituals in central Mexico, where it is offered to the hearth within the sweat bath following the birth of a child, and it also had medicinal uses associated with menstruation, labor, and lactation (Sullivan 1982: 19). Similar uses have been documented for Yucatán as well (19). Additionally, Knowlton and Dzidz Yam (this issue) report that cotton thread is passed over the body of a woman experiencing a difficult labor by ritual healers in certain Yucatec Maya communities today. It may therefore be the case that the close association between the elderly codical goddess named with T1027 and cotton serves as a signifier for her role as a healer, as well as a weaver. This role was assumed by Tlazolteotl-Ixcuina in highland Mexico, the latter a deity of Huastec origin whose name means "Lady Cotton." This epithet also appears quite apt for the elderly deity under discussion.

## Discussion and Conclusions

This survey of midwifery practices in Maya cultures demonstrates the continued importance of key elements across time, although they appear to have persisted to a greater degree in the Maya highlands, as opposed to the lowlands, where steam bathing and a complex of female deities related to weaving, childbirth, and the moon retain their significance in certain communities, among them Santiago Atitlán. While there has clearly been substantial Christian influence in terms of certain aspects (such as the name associated with the female deity complex), comparisons with the pre-Hispanic Maya codices reveal a number of similarities that speak of a broad set of beliefs that appears to have spanned the highland and lowland Maya regions, and perhaps even farther afield.

The commonalities that are most striking are those that link weaving activities with pregnancy and childbirth; the personification of the warping board and loom; the links between women (midwives especially), serpents, and otherworldly realms; and complexes of female deities with aspects that encompass different age grades, pairings with male counterparts, and, most likely, seasonal cycles. Additionally, objects and iconography related to women and birth—in the form of serpents, umbilical cords, and ropes—tie this act to primordial creation events and highlight the association between midwife and creator grandmother.

This analysis further clarifies the role of the female Maya codical deities—young and old, human-like and bestial in aspect—suggesting that they had separate albeit overlapping associations. While Chak Chel is most commonly associated with rain and storm waters, the goddess named by T1027 appears to play a more consistent role as an elderly female associated with the care of women and children, and as the one giving birth to cloth. Ethnohistoric sources suggest, however, that a much broader complex of female deities existed at the time, one that is slowly being teased out by studies such as these reported in this special issue of *Ethnohistory*.

## Notes

I appreciate the invitation by Rebecca Dufendach to participate in this special issue of *Ethnohistory*. I have enjoyed collaborating with her and the other contributors and found their feedback and suggestions on an earlier draft of my article to be extremely valuable. I also would like to thank William Duncan and Christine Hernández for engaging discussions on the topics addressed as well as their feedback on earlier drafts of this work and the anonymous reviewers for their comments, which proved very helpful in revising my earlier manuscript. I also appreciate the professionalism and dedication of the *Ethnohistory* staff and, in particular, John Schwaller's generous contribution toward the reproduction of images from the codices.

1  Yaxper is a member of the María complex, a grouping of deities that serve as the female principle and also represent the moon, the twelve months of the year, Lake Atitlán, and the parts of the loom. A thirteenth María (discussed below), known as Francisca Batz'bal, stands apart from the others. She is linked to the Mam, who is associated with sterility and the dry season.

2  This concept may have an analogue in the Postclassic Maya codices. In the register illustrating the ceremonies at the start of the new year in the Dresden Codex (on pages 25–28), a loincloth with footprints worn by representations of the four directional world trees signifies the passage of time during the year.

3  Repositioning a breech infant through massage is an important role of midwives in other parts of the Maya area as well. Midwives also use massage for other purposes, such as relieving back and leg pain, easing delivery, and repositioning the uterus following childbirth (Kunow 2003: 51).

4  The steam bath is thought of as the earth's womb. It has associations with Francisca Batz'bal and is also where the Mam is said to sleep (Tarn and Prechtel 1986: 178).

5  *Ixcuina* is a Huastec term meaning "Lady of Cotton"; *Ix-* is the female marker, and *cuinim* means "cotton" (Larson 1955, cited in Sullivan 1982: 12).

6  Battens are sometimes used as weapons by female warrior deities, based on the belief that women undergoing childbirth were like warriors on the field of battle (Sullivan 1982: 17–18).

7  Note that these mirror, in many respects, the implements associated with the deities in the Tlazolteotl-Ixcuina complex.

8  Her name remains difficult to translate. *Ix-* is the female prefix, and *woh* refers to "glyphs," but I have not found a meaning for *asal* that makes sense in this context.

9  The reference to the wives of the physicians and sorcerers recalls almanacs in the Maya codices in which certain female activities, such as weaving and sewing,

are said to be undertaken by "the wife of X male deity" (Vail and Stone 2002). In the context of the Sip ritual, I wonder if what is implicit in Landa's description is the fact that the women attending are the "sorceresses" (i.e., midwives). I also wonder, based on research by Edward Polanco (2018) pertaining to Nahuatl culture, if the designation "midwife" for indigenous female medical practitioners obscured the fact that the women so described were trained in and performed the same range of diagnostic and healing rituals as their male counterparts.

10 This ritual is discussed in more detail in the section on pre-Hispanic midwifery practices below, as an example of this ceremony appears to be included in the *Madrid Codex*.

11 The term *chel* has not been satisfactorily translated in this context. It is most commonly given as "rainbow" (see Thompson 1970, 1972) but may also be related to the word for 'tree' (*che'*). Such an interpretation would fit well with Tz'utujiil beliefs about the mother tree from which all life is said to come.

12 In the latter aspect, she might be compared to Francisca Batz'bal.

13 Cords suspended from the sky occur in several different contexts in the Maya codices, where they are associated with the birth of deities and/or celestial beings, such as the sun. In one scene from the *Paris Codex*, they wind around a set of quadripartite deities known as Pawahtuns (or alternately as variants of the creator Itzamna). Scholars associate these figures with the Mam deities found among Maya groups in Belize and Guatemala. In some areas they are quadripartite aspects of a single deity, and in others there is only one Mam (Taube 1992:97). The Mam(s)—so important in beliefs and rituals associated with childbirth among the Tz'utujiil Maya—also appear on the Birth Vase, in association with Chak Chel.

14 Note that the word *kab'* refers to "bees, beehives, and honey" and also to "earth." Beehives are marked by multiple *kab'* glyphs in the Madrid Codex to signify this connection. It may also be significant that the stingless bee kept by Yucatec Maya cultures, known as *xunan kab'*, is conceptualized as female, as opposed to other types of stingless bees, which are identified as male.

15 This may signify a dichotomy similar to that seen among the Mam and Martín of the contemporary Tz'utujiil, who represent the contrast between the wet (Martín) and dry (Mam) seasons (Christenson 2001).

16 It has also been suggested that, rather than water, what is portrayed is amniotic fluid (Brisko 1994).

17 Only the second of the four female deities depicted has the defining attributes (a wrinkled face and single tooth in the lower jaw) of old age.

18 Although her name glyph is not included here, it is given in the following almanac (*Madrid Codex* 102c), which pictures the same figure.

19 Chaak, rather than Itzamna, is named in the text, however.

20 It is of interest that she takes the (*y*)-*al* ("her child") attributive in the almanac on page 107b of the beekeeping section in the *Madrid Codex*.

## References

Báez-Jorge, Félix. 1983. "La cosmovisión de los zoques de Chiapas." In *Antropología e Historia de los mixe-zoque y los mayas*, edited by Lorenzo Ochoa and Thomas A. Lee. Jr., 383–411. Mexico City and Provo, UT: Universidad Nacional Autónoma de Mexico and Brigham Young University.

Batún Alpuche, Adolfo Iván, Patricia A. McAnany, and Maia Dedrick. 2017. "Tiempo y paisaje en Tahcabo, Yucatán." *Arqueología Mexicana* 146: 66–71.

Brasseur de Bourbourg, Charles E. 1869–70. *Etudes sur le système graphique et la langue des Mayas.* Paris: Impériale.

Brisko, Joann R. 1994. "Maya Goddesses: By What Name Do We Call Them?" In *U Mut Maya V*, edited by Carolyn Jones and Tom Jones, 197–206. Arcata, CA: U Mut Maya.

Christenson, Allen J. 2001. *Art and Society in a Highland Maya Community: The Altarpiece of Santiago Atitlan.* Austin: University of Texas Press.

Chuchiak, John. 2004. "Papal Bulls, Extirpators, and the Madrid Codex: The Content and Probable Provenience of the M. 56 Patch." In *The Madrid Codex: New Approaches to Understanding an Ancient Maya Manuscript*, edited by Gabrielle Vail and Anthony Aveni, 57–88. Boulder: University Press of Colorado.

Ciaramella, Mary. 1994. "The Lady with the Snake Headdress." In *Seventh Palenque Round Table, 1989*, edited by Merle Greene Robertson and Virginia M. Fields, 201–09. San Francisco: Pre-Columbian Art Research Institute.

Ciudad Real, Antonio de. 2001. *Calepino Maya de Motul*, edited by René Acuña. Mexico City: Plaza y Valdes.

*Codex Borgia.* 1963. *Codex Borgia, Biblioteca Apostolica Vaticana, Rome.* Mexico City: Fondo de Cultura Económica.

*Codex Tudela.* 1980. *Códice Tudela.* Madrid: Ediciones Cultura Hispanica.

Corona Núñez, José. 1964–67. *Antigüedades de Mexico basadas en la recopilación de Lord Kingsborough.* 4 vols. Mexico City: Secretaría de Hacienda y Crédito Público.

Cosminsky, Sheila. 2001. "Maya Midwives of Southern Mexico and Guatemala." In *Mesoamerican Healers*, edited by Brad R. Huber and Alan R. Sandstrom, 179–212. Austin: University of Texas Press.

Duncan, William N., and Charles Andrew Hofling. 2011. "Why the Head? Cranial Modification as Protection and Ensoulment among the Maya." *Ancient Mesoamerica* 22, no. 1: 199–210.

Durán, Diego. 1971. *Book of the Gods and Rites of the Ancient Calendar*, translated by Fernando Horcasitas and Doris Heyden. Norman: University of Oklahoma Press.

Fenton, William N. 1957. *American Indian and White Relations to 1830: Needs and Opportunities for Study.* Chapel Hill: University of North Carolina Press.

Fenton, William N. 1966. "Field Work, Museum Studies, and Ethnohistorical Research." In *Ethnohistory* 13, no. 1/2: 71–85.

Förstemann, Ernst. 1880. *Die Maya Handschrift der Königlichen öffentlichen Bibliothek zu Dresden.* Leipzig, Germany: A. Naumannschen Lichtdruckeret.

Fuentes y Guzmán, Francisco de. 1969–72. *Obras históricas de don Francisco Antonio de Fuentes y Guzmán: Recordación Florida (1690–1699)*, edited by Carmelo Sáenz de Santa María. 3 vols. Madrid: Ediciones Atlas.

García de Palacio, Diego. 1927. "Relación hecha por el Licenciado Palacio al Rey D. Felipe II, en la que describe la provincia de Guatemala, las costumbres de los indios y otras cosas notables (1574)." *Anales de la Sociedad de Geografía e Historia de Guatemala* 4: 71–92.

Garibay K., Angel María. 1967. "Códice Carolino." *Estudios de cultura náhuatl* 7: 12–58.

Groark, Kevin P. 1997. "To Warm the Blood, To Warm the Flesh: The Role of the Steambath in Highland Maya (Tzeltal-Tzotzil) Ethnomedicine." *Journal of Latin American Lore* 20, no. 1: 3–96.

Hanks, William F. 1990. *Referential Practice: Language and Lived Space among the Maya.* Chicago: University of Chicago Press.

Hernández, Francisco. 1959. *Historia natural de Nueva España.* 5 vols. Mexico City: Universdad Nacional Autónoma de Mexico.

Ichon, Alain. 1973. "La religion de los Totonacas de la sierra." Colección Sepini 16. Mexico City: Instituto Nacional Indígenista.

Jong, Harriet J. de. 1999. *The Land of Corn and Honey: The Keeping of Stingless Bees (meliponiculture) in the Ethno-Ecological Environment of Yucatan (Mexico) and El Salvador.* PhD diss., Universiteit Utrecht.

Kingsborough, Edward King, Viscount. 1831. Vol. 3 of *Antiquities of Mexico: Comprising Fac-Similes of Ancient Mexican Paintings and Hieroglyphics, Preserved in the Royal Libraries of Paris, Berlin, and Dresden; in the Imperial Library of Vienna; in the Vatican Library; in the Borgian Museum at Rome; in the Library of the Institute at Bologna; and in the Bodleian Library at Oxford. Together with the Monuments of New Spain, by M. Dupaix, With Their Respective Scales of Measurement and Accompanying Descriptions. The Whole Illustrated by Many Valuable Inedited Manuscripts, by Lord Kingsborough. The Drawings, on Stone, by A. Aglio.* 9 vols. London: Robert Havell and Colnaghi, Son, and Co.

Klein, Cecelia. 1975. "Post-Classic Mexican Death Imagery as a Sign of Cyclical Completion." In *Death and the Afterlife in Pre-Columbian America*, edited by Elizabeth P. Benson, 69–86. Washington, DC: Dumbarton Oaks.

Klein, Cecelia. 1982. "Woven Heaven, Tangled Earth: A Weaver's Paradigm of the Mesoamerican Cosmos." In *Ethnohistory and Archaeoastronomy in the American Tropics*, edited by Anthony F. Aveni and Gary Urton, 1–36. New York: New York Academy of Sciences.

Knowlton, Timothy. 2016. "Filth and Healing in Yucatan: Interpreting Ix Hun Ahau, a Maya Goddess." *Ancient Mesoamerica* 27, no. 2: 319–32.

Kunow, Marianna A. 2003. *Maya Medicine: Traditional Healing in Yucatán.* Albuquerque: University of New Mexico Press.

Larson, Ramón. 1955. Vocabulario huasteco del Estado de San Luis Potosí. Mexico City: Instituto Lingüistico de Verano and Secretaría de Educación Pública.

Las Casas, Bartolomé de. 1967. *Apologética historia sumaria*, edited by Edmundo O'Gorman. 2 vols. Mexico City: Insituto de Investigaciones Históricas, Universidad Autónoma de Mexico.

López de Cogolludo, Diego. (1688) 1955. *Historia de Yucatán.* 3 vols. Mexico City: Editorial Academia Literaria.

Martínez, Maximino. 1944. *Las plantas medicinales de Mexico.* Mexico City: Ediciones Botas.

Mellen, George-Ann. 1974. "El uso de las plantas medicinales en Guatemala." *Guatemala Indígena* 9, no. 12: 99–179.

Mendelson, E. Michael. 1957. *Religion and World-View in a Guatemalan Village.* Manuscripts on Middle American Cultural Anthropology, Microfilm Collection, no. 52. Chicago: University of Chicago Library.

Milbrath, Susan. 1995. "Gender and Roles of Lunar Deities in Postclassic Central Mexico and Their Correlations with the Maya Area." *Estudios de Cultural Nahuatl* 25: 45–93.

Miller, Mary, and Karl Taube. 1993. *An Illustrated Dictionary of the Gods and Symbols of Ancient Mexico and the Maya*. New York and London: Thames and Hudson.

Moyes, Holly. 2005. "The Sweatbath in the Cave: A Modified Passage in Chechem Ha Cave, Belize." In *Stone Houses and Earth Lords: Maya Religion in the Cave Context*, edited by Keith M. Prufer and James E. Brady, 187–212. Boulder: University Press of Colorado.

Nicholson, Henry B. 1971. "Religion in Pre-Hispanic Central Mexico." In *Archaeology of Northern Mesoamerica, Part 1*, edited by Gordon Ekholm and Ignacio Bernal, vol. 10 of *Handbook of Middle American Indians*, edited by Robert Wauchope, 395–446. Austin: University of Texas Press.

Ossado, Ricardo. 1834. "Medicina doméstica: descripción de los nombres y virtudes de las yerbas indígenas de Yucatán." Unpublished ms., Mérida, Mexico.

Orellana, Sandra. 1987 *Indian Medicine in Highland Guatemala: The Prehispanic and Colonial Periods*. Albuquerque: University of New Mexico Press.

Polanco, Edward A. 2018. "'I Am Just a Tiçitl': Decolonizing Central Mexican Nahua Female Healers, 1535–1635." *Ethnohistory* 65, no. 3: 441–63.

Prechtel, Martin, and Robert S. Carlsen. 1988. "Weaving and Cosmos amongst the Tzutujil Maya of Guatemala." *Res: Anthropology and Aesthetics* 15: 122–32.

Redfield, Robert, and Alfonso Villa Rojas. 1934. *Chan Kom: A Maya Village*. Publication No. 448. Washington, DC: Carnegie Institution of Washington.

Rosny, Léon de. 1888. *Codex Peresianus. Manuscrit hiératique des anciens Indiens de l'Amérique Centrale, conservé a la Biblithèque nationale de Paris*. Paris: Bureau de la Société Américane.

Sahagún, Fray Bernardino de. 1950–82. *Florentine Codex: General History of the Things of New Spain*. 12 vols. Translated and annotated by Charles E. Dibble and Arthur J. O. Anderson. Santa Fe and Provo: School of American Research and the University of Utah Press.

Saville, Marshall H. 1921. "Reports on the Maya Indians of Yucatan by Santiago Mendez, Antonio García y Cubas, Pedro Sanchez de Aguilar, and Francisco Hernandez." In *Indian Notes and Monographs* 9: 133–226. New York: Museum of the American Indian.

Scholes, France V., and Eleanor Adams. 1938. *Don Diego Quijada, alcalde mayor de Yucatán, 1561–1565: Documentos sacados de los Archivos de España*. Mexico City: Antigua Libreria Robredo, de José Porrúa e Hijos.

Seler, Eduard. 1960–61. *Gesammelte Abhandlungen zur Amerikanischen Sprach- und Altertumskunde*. 5 vols. Graz, Austria: Akademische Druck-und Verlagsanstalt.

Stone, Andrea. 1995. *Images from the Underworld: Naj Tunich and the Tradition of Maya Cave Painting*. Austin: University of Texas Press.

Stone, Andrea. 1999. "Architectural Innovation in the Temple of the Warriors at Chichén Itzá." In *Mesoamerican Architecture as a Cultural Symbol*, edited by Jeff K. Kowalski, 298–319. New York: Oxford University Press.

Sullivan, Thelma D. 1982. "Tlazolteotl-Ixcuina: The Great Spinner and Weaver." In *The Art and Iconography of Late Post-Classic Central Mexico*, edited by Elizabeth H. Boone, 7–35. Washington, DC: Dumbarton Oaks.

Tarn, Nathaniel, and Martin Prechtel. 1986. "Constant Inconstancy: The Feminine Principle in Atiteco Mythology." In *Symbol and Meaning beyond the Closed*

*Community: Essays in Mesoamerican Ideas*, edited by Gary H. Gossen, 173–84. Albany: Institute for Mesoamerican Studies, State University of New York.

Taube, Karl A. 1994. "The Birth Vase: Natal Imagery in Ancient Maya Myth and Ritual." In vol. 4 of *Maya Vase Book*, edited by Justin Kerr, 650–85. New York: Kerr Associates.

Thompson, J. Eric S. 1939. "The Moon Goddess in Middle America with Notes on Related Deities." In *Contributions to American Anthropology and History*, vol. 5, no. 29, 121–73. Washington, DC: Carnegie Institution of Washington.

Thompson, J. Eric S. 1970. *Maya History and Religion*. Norman: University of Oklahoma Press.

Thompson, J. Eric S. 1972. *A Commentary on the Dresden Codex: A Maya Hieroglyphic Book*. Vol. 93 of *Memoirs of the American Philosophical Society*. Philadelphia: American Philosophical Society.

Torquemada, Fray Juan de. 1943. *Monarquía Indiana*. 3 vols. Mexico City: Biblioteca Porrúa.

Tozzer, Alfred M. 1941. *Landa's relación de las cosas de Yucatan*. Vol. 18 of *Papers of the Peabody Museum of American Archaeology and Ethnology*. Cambridge, MA: Harvard University.

Vail, Gabrielle, and Andrea Stone. 2002. "Representations of Women in Postclassic and Colonial Maya Literature and Art." In *Ancient Maya Women*, edited by Traci Ardren, 203–28. Walnut Creek, CA: Alta Mira Press.

Vail, Gabrielle, and Christine Hernández. 2012. "Rain and Fertility Rituals in Postclassic Yucatan Featuring Chaak and Chak Chel." In *The Ancient Maya of Mexico: Reinterpreting the Past of the Northern Maya Lowlands*, edited by Geoffrey E. Braswell, 285–305. Sheffield, UK: Equinox.

Villacorta Cifuentes, Jorge Luís. 1976. *Historia de la medicina, cirugia y obstetrician prehispanicas*. Guatemala City: self-published.

Wagley, Charles. 1949. *The Social and Religious Life of a Guatemalan Village*. Menosha, WI: American Anthropological Association.

Wisdom, Charles. 1940. *The Chortí Indians of Guatemala*. Chicago: University of Chicago Press.

# Perinatal Rites in the *Ritual of the Bacabs,* a Colonial Maya Manuscript

Timothy W. Knowlton, *Berry College*
Edber Dzidz Yam, *Centro de Investigaciones y Estudios Superiores en Antropología Social*

**Abstract.** Pregnancy and childbirth were among indigenous Maya women's most dangerous life experiences, with very high maternal and perinatal death rates from pre-Hispanic times through the first decades of the twentieth century. This article contributes to the knowledge of colonial Yucatec Maya women through the interpretation of documentary evidence of three indigenous rites meant to facilitate women's perinatal health and successful childbirth. This evidence is contained in the eighteenth-century collection of healing chants known as the "ritual of the bacabs." The chants include those for cooling the steam bath used in indigenous perinatal treatments, for difficulty in childbirth, and for rites surrounding the disposal of the afterbirth. Through an analysis that combines philological approaches with ethnographic interviews of contemporary Maya speakers, this article provides new insights into the intersection between ritual and culture-specific notions of the body among the colonial Maya.

**Keywords.** Maya, childbirth, ritual, ethnomedicine

## Introduction

Several decades of scholarship has elucidated many aspects of the childbirth experiences of indigenous women in pre-Hispanic and colonial Latin American societies (e.g., Bruhns and Stothert 2014; Kellogg 2005; Socolow 2015), including the Maya women of Yucatàn (Chuchiak 2007; Restall 1995; Vail and Stone 2002). However, given the patriarchal social conditions of the colonial epoch and the resulting lacunae in the documentary record, our knowledge of colonial Maya women's experiences is incomplete.

*Ethnohistory* 66:4 (October 2019)  DOI 10.1215/00141801-7683312
Copyright 2019 by American Society for Ethnohistory

As in the case of colonial Nahua women in Central Mexico (Polanco 2018), we know little of Yucatec Maya women's roles and experiences in the domain of indigenous healing. Furthermore, pregnancy and childbirth were among women's most dangerous life experiences, with very high maternal and perinatal death rates from pre-Hispanic times through the first decades of the twentieth century (Sesia 2016). Even today, living at the intersection of social and gender-based inequalities, indigenous Maya women are at substantially higher risk of maternal death in Yucatán (Rodríguez Angulo, Andueza-Pech, and Oliva Peña 2018). This article contributes to our knowledge of colonial Yucatec Maya women through the interpretation of documentary evidence of three indigenous rites meant to facilitate women's perinatal health and successful childbirth.

Documentary evidence of the three perinatal rites under discussion appears in the colonial manuscript known to scholars as the *Ritual of the Bacabs* (Arzápalo Marín 1987; Roys 1965). This manuscript is among the richest Maya-language sources on rites relating to the human body. Maya treatments (both then and now) include combinations of herbal decoctions, physical manipulation of the patient's body, and ritual chants. The *Ritual of the Bacabs* is a colonial compilation of these healing chants and some herbal remedies, written in Yucatec Maya using a modified alphabetic script introduced by the Spanish. Although the extant manuscript dates to the late eighteenth century, the healing lore within it bridges pre-Hispanic epigraphic records and the reports of later ethnographers working in Maya communities. Scholars have long recognized these esoteric chants as among the most important, yet notoriously difficult, sources of Maya culture to interpret (Thompson 1970; Houston et al. 2009: 28). The chants are notable for the prominent roles of pre-Hispanic Maya goddesses (Knowlton 2015a; 2016) and for their use of archaic metaphors that appear in those Classic period (AD 250–900) hieroglyphic inscriptions that describe the conjuring of divine forces (Knowlton 2010; 2012).

As Matthew Restall (2003: 124–25) has noted, developments in Maya epigraphy in recent decades enable the colonial Maya ethnohistorian to not simply "upstream" from modern ethnographic data, but also to move forward to the colonial period from pre-Hispanic sources. With the eighteenth-century manuscript as our datum, we employ a similar methodology here as well. In contrast with similar texts collected in the course of ethnographic research (e.g., Levi-Strauss 1950), the chants accompanying colonial Maya perinatal rites apparently were written by indigenous healers for indigenous healers in a context historically distant from our own. Therefore, we employ a mixed methodology that combines textual analysis of a colonial Maya language manuscript with data from key consultant interviews with contemporary Yucatec Maya healers (*h menob*) as well as free list interviews (Quinlin 2005) with a stratified sample of Maya laypeople. This is done to enrich our interpretation of otherwise esoteric texts by providing the necessary contextual information not fully accessible in the extant historical record.

We argue that the *Ritual of the Bacabs* is one of our best Maya sources for indigenous rites surrounding childbirth, even though it has not always been recognized as such. We assert that manuscript pages 174–89 contain three distinct chants directed at three different concerns regarding childbirth, although only one of these three has been consistently recognized as dealing with perinatal rites. The pioneering ethnohistorian Ralph Roys (1965) noted in his English translation of the work that the chant on manuscript pages 174–80 accompanied a ritual for the afterbirth, yet he misidentified the purpose of the two other chants following it. For example, Karl A. Taube (1998: 439) recognized that the chant on manuscript pages 180–83, which Roys had identified as being for cooling a pit oven, is in fact for cooling a steam bath (both of which during colonial times were called *pib*).[1] Steam baths were important structures in traditional Mesoamerican healing traditions, including for treating women giving birth. As Stephen D. Houston (1996) has demonstrated, the cognate term *pibnah* appears in classic Maya epigraphic texts referring to archaeological structures functioning (actually or symbolically) as steam baths. And as we will argue in this article, a third chant (ms. pp. 183–89) is also for treating a complication during childbirth. In total, these three chants provide a unique insight into the relationship between the work of ritual healers (*h menob*) and midwives treating women during the colonial period in Yucatán. Furthermore, we hope that the results of this analysis demonstrate the productivity of a mixed methods approach to ethnohistoric reconstruction and interpretation.

## Steam Bathing in Colonial Perinatal Rites

The first chant we will discuss begins on manuscript page 180, where it is labeled by the scribe as *v thanil u siscunabal pib lae*, "This is the word for the cooling of a *pib*." Sweat baths are an important feature of autochthonous Mesoamerican medical systems, and their use was prescribed in some colonial Maya remedies (Gubler 2018: 117). Although no longer in regular use in Yucatán today, at least two forms of sweat-bath structures are known from the early seventeenth-century Motul dictionary of the Yucatec Maya language. The first was a more temporary structure called *puc na che*, defined in the Motul (Ciudad Real 2001: 512) as "a little hut made of cane so as to take sweats in it" ("chozilla hecha de varas como para tomar sudores en ella"). This description parallels the wattle-and-daub steam baths still in use in some Tzeltal Maya communities in Chiapas (Groark 1997: 30–31). A second, more permanent structure was known as the *pib*. Today in Yucatec, *pib* refers only to the pit oven in which ritual foodstuffs are cooked, but in colonial times it also referred to the "bath or *temazcal* in which those women who are about to give birth or who had recently given birth are purified" ("baño o temazcal en que se purificaban las parturientas o recién paridas"; Ciudad Real 2001: 491).

The text of the chant for the steam bath includes a description of dousing heated rocks counterclockwise in the four cardinal directions (indicated by their respective color symbolism) to generate steam for heating and purifying women's bodies during perinatal rites:

| | |
|---|---|
| oxlahun pul bacin yn ɔonotil ha | Thirteen pitchers of my cenote water evidently,[2] |
| oxlahun pis yn [181] batil ha | Thirteen measures of my hail-stone water |
| oc ti zintunil | enter the steam bath stone. |
| same tun ualaccen t u pach chac munyal yk | Already then I may stand behind the red cloud wind; |
| [sa]me tun ualaccen t uu ich sac munyal yk | Already then I may stand facing the white cloud wind; |
| same tun ualaccen t uu ich ek munyal yk | Already then I may stand facing the black cloud wind; |
| \same tun ualaccen t uu ich kan munyal yk | Already then I may stand facing the yellow cloud wind. |

(*Ritual of the Bacabs* ca. 1779: 180–81. All translations by Timothy W. Knowlton unless otherwise noted.)

Furthermore, the chant closes with what, when properly translated, is a recognizable metaphorical description of birth that corresponds with pre-Hispanic imagery:

| | |
|---|---|
| colpay tun bacin [183] yn cah ti x um xuchit | I forcefully remove the flower bud then evidently. |
| pa a chi yɮam | Open your mouth, Itzam! |
| he tun ɮilil | Here is the unchaste woman then. |

(*Ritual of the Bacabs* ca. 1779: 183.)

One area in which the *Ritual of the Bacabs* departs from contemporary Maya healing chants ethnographers have documented is in the frequent reference to pre-Hispanic deities, many of which have since been replaced

Figure 1a.   Classic Maya birth scene on ceramic vase with aged god emerging from a gaping reptilian mouth (K1198; research.mayavase.com/kerrmaya.html; Photograph copyright by Justin Kerr; used with permission).

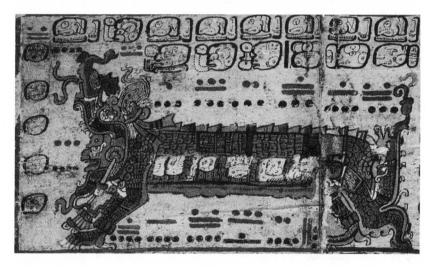

Figure 1b.   The aged god Itzamna emerges from the gaping maw of a reptilian being (*Dresden Codex* 4b).

by Christian saints (with the exception of the Chac storm gods). In this chant, the image of the crocodilian god Itzam's open mouth suggests the common birth scenes of deities emerging from gaping reptilian jaws found in much earlier classic Maya iconography (Taube 1994; fig. 1a) on through the Postclassic period (fig. 1b).

Although today steam baths are no longer used in Yucatec Maya perinatal rituals (Jordan 1993), there remains a concern with the physiology of expectant mothers both before and after childbirth. In our own conversations with contemporary Maya healers, for example, children born on the spiritually significant days of Tuesday or Friday are thought to possess a "force" that Maya people call *kinam*. In Yucatec Maya, the term *kinam* often describes kinds of pain felt in the body. In their dictionary of the contemporary Yucatec Maya language spoken in Hocabá, Victoria Bricker, Eleuterio Po'ot Yah, and Ofelia Dzul de Po'ot (1998: 153) define *kinam* as "pain" of an aching or throbbing character. In interviews conducted by Dzidz Yam in January 2017, Maya speakers distinguish numerous subtypes of kinam pains depending on the location and character of the harm, including "burning" (*eelel*), "shocking" (*léemléem*), and "stinging" (*t'óot'och*) varieties.

Beyond referencing pain, however, *kinam* refers to a broader ethnophysiological concept of the variable quality of things, with certain objects and living beings having greater kinam than others (Villa Rojas 1980; Ciudad Real 2001: 336; Knowlton 2018). Among the twentieth-century Maya of Quintana Roo, community leaders and individuals known to possess kinam were the ones chosen to operate the fire drill during the New Fire ceremony (Villa Rojas 1945: 122). The proximity of persons with relatively stronger or weaker kinam is an important concern. For example, proper marriage partners should be of comparable "heat" or else one of the spouses will become sick (Redfield and Villa Rojas 1934: 163; Villa Rojas 1945: 133).

To help resolve ambiguities in the documentary and ethnographic record, Dzidz Yam conducted free list interviews in January 2017 in Yucatán about what causes kinam in a person. Respondents composed a stratified sample of thirty male and female Maya speakers between the ages of twenty and sixty-four from the community of Yaxunah (population 637). The transcriptions were subsequently analyzed by Knowlton using Visual Anthropac software (Analytic Technologies 2003) to determine the frequency and salience of items in the freelists (Bernard and Ryan 2010). Important kinam-causing items included exposure to sexual activity, to the sun, to excessive cold (*pasmo*) or heat, to domestic animals, to winds, and to cemeteries. However, by far the most frequent and salient cause listed was exposure to pregnant women (figs 2a and 2b).[3]

The managing of pregnancy before and after childbirth is not only a concern for the pregnant women but for those members of the community in proximity to her in her body's charged state. Therefore perhaps it is unsurprising that the *Ritual of the Bacabs* contains more materials pertaining to perinatal rites than had been recognized by scholars previously, but which a mixed methodology makes more apparent.

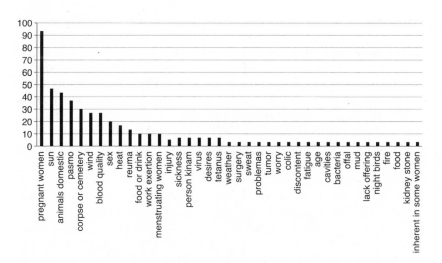

Figure 2a.   Causes of *kinam* among Yaxunah respondents, by frequency

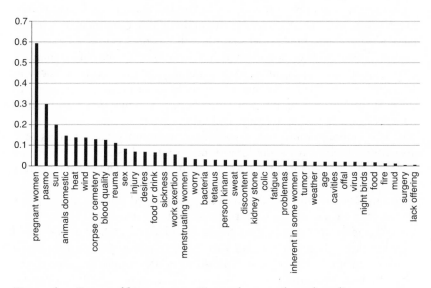

Figure 2b.   Causes of *kinam* among Yaxunah respondents, by salience

## Midwifery in *Ritual of the Bacabs*

Maya midwives have assisted births since pre-Hispanic times (Landa [ca. 1566] 1978: 56; Taube 1994). Attempts by the state to regulate midwives in what is today Mexico began as early as the late eighteenth century, although success was limited until the second half of the twentieth century (Sesia 2016). Biomedical intervention in childbirth in Yucatec Maya communities has increased substantially since the late 1990s (Veile and Kramer 2018), and contemporary Maya midwifery undoubtedly has been transformed by training courses and certification programs conducted by Mexican public health authorities (Güémez Pineda et al. n.d.). Nonetheless, we have found that even where coordination between midwives and *h menob* ("ritual healers") has declined, memories of previous concepts and practices remain.

According to our contemporary Maya consultants, kinam is an important consideration in birth rites and the practice of midwives. For example, the excessive kinam of children born on Tuesday or Friday can cling to the hands of the midwife by the time she has delivered her thirteenth child. Although not often practiced at present, a cleansing ritual by a h men (ritual healer) can prevent this excess force from being transferred to other pregnant women in the course of the midwife's prenatal massage, to the patient's detriment. One healer described this as the "vapor" (*y oxol*) and "smoke" (*u buɔil*) of the kinam, which remains on the hands of the midwife after so many deliveries (interview, 14 January, 2015, Yaxunah, Yucatán, Mexico). As the second colonial chant under discussion demonstrates, in the past this partnership between ritual healers and midwives extended to addressing other perinatal issues, including obstetric crises.

These ethnographic interviews with contemporary Maya healers have also contributed to resolving long-standing misunderstandings about the purpose of some chants in the *Ritual of the Bacabs*. The chant on pages 183–89 is titled *v sihil tok*, which Roys (1965: 61) translated literally as "the birth of the flint" and believed accompanied flint knapping. This interpretation seemed to be supported by the references to *tok* ("flint blade") and *halal* ("reed"), the latter of the kind from which arrow shafts were traditionally made (Ciudad Real 2001: 241). Also occurring in the chant is an invocation of four color-directional butterflies (*pepen*), the butterfly being a martial symbol best known from the arts of Classic and Postclassic Central Mexico (Berlo 1983; Taube 2001). These references to butterflies in the Maya chant are highly unusual for colonial texts, with *pepen* only occuring once in the eight different colonial *Books of Chilam Balam* transcribed by Helga-Maria Miram and Wolfgang Miram (1988: 993).

Nonetheless, the internal location of this chant in the manuscript between two chants related to perinatal rites (pp. 174–83) and two others directed at constipation (pp. 189–206) suggests that the chant might be directed at a complaint regarding the lower body. During our interviews with contemporary Maya healers, we learned that *u sihil tok* can refer to a kind of complication during childbirth. One Maya healer explained to us that in cases of a *tok* birth, the child's head cannot exit because of obstruction by the placenta, perhaps describing the medical condition known as placenta previa.[4] This condition is associated with obstetric hemorrhage and with placenta accreta, major contributors to maternal death among contemporary indigenous women in Mexico and Central America today (Schwartz 2018b: 43–45), and presumably in the past as well.

So what are we to make of the colonial chant? Several of the terms that suggest martial accoutrements also have meanings in the context of midwifery and healing. In ethnographically documented Maya communities, the *halal* reed is traditionally used by the midwife to cut the umbilical cord (Redfield and Villa Rojas 1934: 182). Moreover, *tok* can refer not only to a flint blade but also to a serpent fang or other such lancet used to puncture or let blood (Bricker, Po'ot Yah, and Dzul de Po'ot 1998: 279; Ciudad Real 2001: 552). In the past such lancets may have served as the tool for clearing the obstruction, although our consultant describes using the teeth of a comb to do so in more recent times. And given the frequency of maternal death prior to the twentieth century, the difficulties associated with placenta previa and other obstetric conditions certainly were life-or-death situations. The Mesoamerican notion of the parturient mother as warrior, well documented for Late Post-classic Aztec society (Schwartz 2018a), might help to explain the unusual butterfly imagery peculiar to this colonial chant.

Even in the absence of the identification by our consultants of *u sihil tok* as an obstetric condition, the chant makes reference to several elements of perinatal practices known ethnographically. For example, early in the chant the healer announces:

| | |
|---|---|
| chabtex y uɓil mehene | Engender [2pl] his healthy child, |
| uɓiuile | this blessed one! |
| ca ix u natab cuxanilon [184] | And then he may understand us living things. |
| kamex chab | Receive [2pl] the progeny! |
| y emel tun u chab ti cab | His progeny descends to the earth then. |

(*Ritual of the Bacabs* ca. 1779: 183–84.)

*Kam* ("to receive") can refer to the work of a midwife, called in modern Yucatec "the woman who receives the baby" (in modern orthography: *x k'am chaampal*; Gümez Pineda 2000: 324).[5]

As mentioned previously, an important part of Maya midwifery past and present is the practice of massaging the pregnant woman up until the time the child is born. The final massage involves "manipulating the uterus to its correct position and the baby to its normal position, ready to be born" (Redfield and Villa Rojas 1934: 360). This practice is described in this chant as well:

> he tun bacin cin can uuɔt u      Here then I vigorously bend her
> nak can                          womb.

(*Ritual of the Bacabs* ca. 1779: 183.)

Another documented practice mentioned in the chant is ɔuɔ ("to suck"), the Maya term for the medical practice of cupping (Bricker and Miram 2002: 137). Cupping was part of the medical bloodletting rite (*tok*) of the h men observed by Robert Redfield and Alfonso Villa Rojas (1934: 172–73), which parallels the apparently pre-Hispanic practice of medical bloodletting noticed in the sixteenth century by Bishop Diego de Landa ([ca.1566] 1978: 47). However, twentieth-century Maya midwives practiced cupping on pregnant women without bleeding them (Redfield and Redfield 1940: 71–72), which is perhaps the practice discussed in the chant as well:

> sam yn kamab u kinam          Already I shall receive her *kinam*,
> can pel t u ba yn chacal ba[c] Four times in my own flesh,
> cex can tul ti ku             You four who are gods,
> cex can tul ti bacabe         You four who are skybearers.
> sam tun ualaccen              Already I shall stand up then.
> yn tec ɔuɔte                  I shall suck it rapidly;
> yn kam u kinam                I receive her *kinam*.
> he tun bacin                  Here it is then evidently.
> cen ti ualhi                  It is I who stood.

(*Ritual of the Bacabs* ca. 1779: 186.)

Another relevant association recognized by scholars working with other Mayan language communities (Prechtel and Carlsen 1988) is that of midwifery with weaving. In our interviews with contemporary Maya healers, a h men called in to assist with a difficult childbirth will pass a cotton ball made up of thirteen threads over the body of the pregnant woman (interview, 14 January, 2015, Yaxunah, Yucatán, Mexico). Already by the twentieth century, backstrap loom weaving and its related equipment were much less common in Yucatán than in some other areas with Mayan language speakers. Nonetheless, references to it do appear in these

Figure 3.   The aged midwife goddess Chac Chel weaves using a backstrap loom (*Madrid Codex* 79c).

colonial chants. For example, alongside the reed (*halal*) traditionally used by the midwife to cut the umbilical cord, there is reference to the warping frame (*chuch*; Ciudad Real 2001: 204) used in weaving:

| | |
|---|---|
| bal tun bacin yn halal | What is my reed then evidently? |
| yax kam | It is the first thing received. |
| lay tun bacin u uayasba yn halal | This is the icon of my reed then evidently. |
| bal tun bacin u chuchteil | What is its wooden warping frame then evidently? |
| [198] u natab yn x bolon puc u uayasba u chuchteil | One might understand that my Lady Nine Hills is the icon of its wooden warping frame. |

(*Ritual of the Bacabs* ca. 1779: 197–98.)

Lady Nine Hills is the title of a deity paired with Chacal Ix Chel elsewhere in the manuscript (ms. pp. 12). Ix Chel is the goddess whom Bishop Landa ([ca. 1566] 1978: 56) famously attributed the role of patron of childbirth. The aged midwife version of this goddess, called Chac Chel, appears both in Classic Maya birth scenes (Taube 1994) and engaged in backstrap loom weaving in the Postclassic codices (fig. 3).

The description of Lady Nine Hills as the "icon" (*uayasba*; see Knowlton 2015b, 2018) of the warping frame is reminiscent of the warping boards in human form used by contemporary Tz'utujil Maya people in Santiago Atitlán (Prechtel and Carlsen 1988: 125). Therefore, in this passage we may have a reference in a Maya language manuscript to the practice reported by Bishop Landa ([ca. 1566] 1978: 56), who noted that the "sorceresses" (indigenous midwives) attending a woman placed an image of Ix Chel near her during childbirth.

As we have seen, even when significant elements of past ideas and practices are no longer current (such as the sweat bath and invocation of the pre-Hispanic deities), data from ethnographic interviews can help resolve enduring problems of translation and interpretation. Having established a range of Maya birth rites and practices in the *Ritual of the Bacabs* not previously recognized by scholars, we turn to an extended interpretation of the single chant already known by Roys (1965) to be associated with birth rites, that of manuscript pages 174–80.

### The Chant for the Afterbirth

As previously mentioned, three chants in the *Ritual of the Bacabs* address rites surrounding childbirth. These include a chant for the afterbirth, a chant for cooling a steam bath, and one for difficulty in childbirth. Steam bathing facilitated health by restoring vital heat during and after childbirth. Despite the decline of steam bath use in Yucatán, the maintenance of vital heat during the perinatal period remains a major concern in Maya medicine. As Redfield and Villa Rojas (1934: 181–82) describe for the twentieth-century Maya community of Chan Kom: "The new-born child and the recent mother must be guarded from the various communicable evils, and at the time of birth 'hot' foods and medicines are essential. . . . The midwife may administer 'hot' drinks, or warm the mother's body with a fire, for cold, at this moment of crisis, is very dangerous."

These concerns and related perinatal practices are found in the *Ritual of the Bacabs* as well, in the case of the chant for the *ibin*. According to the Motul dictionary (Ciudad Real 2001: 301), *ibin* means most generically

Figure 4. Traditional three-stone hearth (*koben*) in the residence of a Maya herbalist in Pisté, Yucatán (photograph by Timothy W. Knowlton, 13 June 2013)

"thread or net" (*tela o red*) but also refers to the placenta. The polysemy of this term is probably not circumstantial, given the widespread linking of weaving and reproduction in Mesoamerican thought (Sullivan 1982; Taube 1994; Pretchel and Carlsen 1988). The placenta is subject to fire-related rituals in modern Yucatec Maya communities, as Redfield and Villa Rojas (1934: 182) report: "The afterbirth is either burned or buried; the preferred place in which to dispose of it is under the hearthstones of deserted houses. This practice, also, is a preventative of the danger of 'cold,' for under such an old hearth 'there are many ashes, and if the afterbirth is buried there, the mother is thus warmed.' The same feeling is present if the afterbirth is burned."[6]

As we will discuss, the colonial chant for the afterbirth on mansucript pages 174–80 follows much the same rationale, although the location in the colonial text of the rite may apply equally to a steam bath structure or to the traditional three-stone domestic hearth (fig. 4).

The section begins:

| | |
|---|---|
| u peɔil ybin lae | This is the chant for the afterbirth. |
| — —- | — —- |
| he tun t a nup | Here it is in your spouse then; |
| tun top ǩilil | The unchaste woman gives birth then. |
| max tun bacin u cool cit be | Oh! Who is the mischief of the sire then evidently, |
| u cool akabe | the mischief of this night? |
| yx hun ɔit balche tun bacin | Lady One *ɔit Balche* is the mischief |
| u cool cit | of the sire then evidently, |
| u col akabe | this mischief of night. |

(*Ritual of the Bacabs* ca. 1779: 174.)

The scribe's introductory statement can be taken to mean either that the text is the sung chant for the afterbirth itself, or that it is for the midwife's massage to assist with expelling the afterbirth, as both are called *peɔ* in colonial Maya. The chant proper begins by addressing the husband, who alongside the midwife in Yucatán traditionally accompanies the wife during childbirth (Redfield and Villa Rojas 1934: 181; Villa Rojas 1945: 140).

The pregnant woman is referred to here and elsewhere in the chants as *ǩilil*, which the Motul dictionary glosses as "that which is unwoven, is torn, or for a woman to be corrupted" (Ciudad Real 2001: 165). The obvious reference here in the context of pregnancy is to a woman who is not a virgin. *Top* in contemporary Yucatec is translated as *chingar* ("to fuck") or *nacer* ("to give birth") (Martínez Huchim 2006: 230), although in the second sense of the word it is more often pronounced *top*, which also means "to blossom" as in fruits, flowers, seeds, and even hatching birds' eggs.[7] The divine patroness of the pregnant woman's ailment is Ix Hun ɔit Balche ("Lady of One Long-Thin Balche Tree"). This is a reference to the divine patroness of the balche tree (*Lonchocarpus longistylus* Pittier), the alcoholic drink of which served as a purgative medicine during Maya festivities (Roys 1931: 216), and also invokes its ancient association with both drunkenness and erotic pleasure (Houston, Stuart, and Taube 2006). Following this identification of the pregnant woman and the divine patroness, the chant continues:

| | |
|---|---|
| canchelic tun bacin yn chacal toncuy | My red heel is propped up then evidently, |
| .4. | [white, black, yellow]. |
| la tun bacin tin taccah yalan u homtanil yǩamcab | I placed this beneath Itzamcab's bowels then evidently. |

| | |
|---|---|
| canchelic tun bacin yn met | My trivet is propped up then evidently. |
| u met y it yn cat xani [175] | Its trivet is the base for my cooking jar also. |
| hunac pecni | Greatly she writhed, |
| hunac chibalnici | Greatly she hurt. |
| picchin tun bacin t u ɔulbal | Cast it violently then to its arbor, |
| ti y acantun | to its lamentation stone, |
| tumen u na t u chũ bin kinim | because its mother is at the heater's base reportedly. |
| can kin bin chellan t u chun kinib | Four days [she] reclined at the heater's base |
| tiba t u chah u kinami | as its *kinam* seized her there. |
| picchin bin t u chun chacal chi | Cast it violently to the base of its boiling mouth reportedly, |
| tiba t u chah u kinami [xu] nan xani | as the *kinam* of the lady seized [her] there also. |

(*Ritual of the Bacabs* ca. 1779: 174–75.)

At this point, the chant describes the elements of the healing space. A cooking pot, called the "bowels of Itzamcab," is propped up by a trivet over the fire.[8] The pregnant woman is described as reclining near the "heater" (*kinib*), which is either the hearth or steam bath fire heating her body during the course of her ordeal. The healer orders her or his tutelary spirits (presumably the Bacabs evoked in other chants) to expel the cause of the sickness from the patient and into elements of the ritual space, such as an altar, or "lamentation stone" (*acantun*), and the arbor (*ɔulbal*), the latter still constructed over the offering table during some rituals in Yucatàn today.

Being near the fire is a means of helping reinforce the health of the woman who has given birth by "heating" her, as discussed above. Likewise, the woman is given "hot" drinks to reinforce her health, in this case "boiled chocolate honey":

| | |
|---|---|
| bal tun bacin u uayasba u cabil yn ci | Then what evidently is the icon of my pulque's honey? |
| chacal chocuah [176] cab u uayasba u cabil yn ci | The boiled chocolate honey is the icon of my pulque's honey; |
| chac bolay | It is the jaguar. |
| tux bacin yn uayasba | Where evidently is my icon |
| ca t ualhen yn tackabte u homtanil yȝaamcab [a]yn | as I stood that I might touch Itzamcab Crocodilian's bowels? |

(*Ritual of the Bacabs* ca. 1779: 175–76.)

The *chacal cocuah cab* ("boiled chocolate honey") undoubtedly refers to the honey that "sweetens the chocolate [drink] given to mothers after childbirth" (Villa Rojas 1945: 58, 141; see also Redfield and Villa Rojas 1934: 183). In the colonial text, the chocolate is called the "jaguar" (*chac bolay*). This recalls a comparable passage in the *Book of Chilam Balam* of Chumayel that identifies the chac bolay and chocolate with the *balamte* (Roys 1933: 36, 111). The balamte is a particular "wild" variant of cacao that is sometimes used as well (*Theobroma bicolor* Bonpl.; Kufer and McNeil 2006). The chocolate drink is prepared with boiled water, and Betty Bernice Faust (1998: 616) notes in the context of a contemporary Maya ritual that the frothing of the chocolate with a special stick is occasioned by jokes about its similarity to sexual intercourse.

Furthermore, the chant contains multiple invocations of biting insects such as *ku sinic* ants and several kinds of wasps:

| | |
|---|---|
| picchin tun bacin y icnal u yum | Cast it violently then in the presence of its father evidently, |
| chacal ku sinic | the red *ku* ant, |
| .4. | [white, black, yellow], |
| ti bin t u chah u chibali | when the biting pain seized [her] there reportedly. |
| ... | ... |
| oxlahun ꝁucech t a ba | You divided yourself into thirteen parts, |
| cech chacal kanale | you who are the red *kanal* wasp, |
| sacal kanale | white *kanal* wasp. |
| oxlahhun ꝁucech t a ba | You divided yourself into thirteen parts |
| cech ah chuctie | you who are this *ah chucti* wasp, |
| sacal ah chuctie | this white *ah chucti* wasp, |
| cech ah chucuke | you who are this *ah chucuk* wasp, |
| cech chacal tupchace | you who are this red *tupchac* wasp, |
| sacal tupchacce | this white *tupchac* wasp. |

(*Ritual of the Bacabs* ca. 1779: 175, 177.)

E. N. Anderson and Felix Medina Tzuc (2005: 190) report that in contemporary Quintana Roo, these ants and other stinging insects are boiled together with roots of *subin* (*Acacia cornigera*) trees, in whose spines they live, to produce medicines that enhance sexual desire in men and women. Of course, their inclusion in the decoction here ("cast into Itzamcab's bowels") is not so much to induce sexual desire but is part of the general goal of "heating" the woman during and after childbirth, sexual desire being an ethnophysiologically "hot" state (Redfield and Villa Rojas 1934: 168). Stinging insects are also invoked in another perinatal treatment, sweat bathing. Because the sweat bath is no longer used in Yucatán, we lack the kinds of ethnographic descriptions that we have for other elements of perinatal rites. However among Tzeltal Maya communities of Chiapas, wasps and bumblebees are placed in the mud walls of the traditional wattle-and-daub steam bath to insure that the bath "bites" or "stings" those within with sufficient heat (Groark 1997: 33). In the case of the chant here, the biting insects are among the thirteen offering portions cast into the boiling kettle over the flame. The division of offerings into thirteen portions is a common element of Maya healers' rites observed in Yucatàn today by us and others (see Love 2012).

Finally, the fire itself is personified in the ritual space where it receives the offerings:

| | |
|---|---|
| sam tun bacin a chib hun | Already then you bite evidently, One |
| y ahual uinicob | Enemy of the Peoples, |
| cech hunac ah kiname | you who are the great *Kinam*, |
| cech hunac ah chibale | you who are the great Biting Pain. |
| hek satalsat yan can | This is the one who is completely pardoned there in the sky, |
| satalsat yan luum | completely pardoned there on the earth |
| t uu ich hun y ahual uini-cob | in the sight of One Enemy of the Peoples. |
| ... | ... |
| sam tun bacin yn cumcint | Already then I caused Four Enemy of |
| can y ahual kak | Fire to increase evidently |
| y alan u homtanil yȝam-cab xani | beneath Itzamcab's bowels there also. |
| oxlahun ȝucech t a ba tun bacin | You divided yourself thirteen times then evidently, |
| cech x mucuil kuȝ | you who are the buried tobacco, |
| cech tin picchintah ychil u homtanil yȝamcab [a]yn | you who I cast violently into Itzam-cab Crocodilian's bowels. |

(*Ritual of the Bacabs* ca. 1779: 178, 179.)

This personified fire goes by the title of *ahual* ("principal enemy and adversary, who kills and destroys" and "vile thing, hurtful and pernicious") (Ciudad Real 2001: 58). This Yucatec term might be cognate with the Colonial K'iche' term *ajal*, itself a loanword from Chol, meaning "evil spirit" or "demon." In the colonial K'iche' manuscript of the *Popol Vuh*, *ajal* is part of the name of several of the disease-causing lords of the Underworld (Christenson 2007: 116n236; Christenson 2008: 66–67). Like the stinging insects, the fire spirit "bites" the woman who gave birth, and who now is said to be "completely pardoned" in the eyes of this same deity. Recall that the Motul dictionary (Ciudad Real 2001: 491) states that a function of the steam bath was to "purify" those women who had recently given birth, and that is probably what is meant by the "pardon" here.

The healer stokes the fire "beneath Itzamcab's bowels," both heating the woman who gave birth and receiving the thirteen portions of ants and wasps mentioned earlier. In addition to biting insects, thirteen portions of "buried" or "hidden" tobacco (*x mucuil kuţ*) are cast into the fire. Tobacco is widely used in Maya medicine for exorcizing sickness-causing winds (Villa Rojas 1945: 157). Its uses in contemporary Quintana Roo also include serving as a poultice applied to the navels of newborns (Anderson et al. 2003: 172), which may be significant given the topic of this chant. At the same time, Yucatec Maya childbirth rites traditionally involve the cremation or burial of the afterbirth beneath the hearth (Redfield and Villa Rojas 1934: 182). So it is also possible that the buried afterbirth itself is meant (as a *uayasba* ["likeness" or "icon"]) instead of literal tobacco. Indeed, in the orations of Nahuatl midwives that Friar Bernardino de Sahagún recorded, it is said of the newborn boy's umbilical cord to be buried in the battlefield: "With this you shall make yourself an offering. . . . This precious object taken from your body shall be counted as your offering of maguey thorns, tobacco, reeds, pine branches" (Sullivan and Knab 1994: 137). And regarding the umbilical cord of the newborn girl, Sahagún's work reports: "You shall be the covering of ashes that banks the fire, you shall be the three stones on which the cooking pot rests. Here our lord buries you, inters you" (138). In either case, the health of the new mother is facilitated through this cleansing offering.

### Conclusion

We have argued here that the colonial manuscript known as the *Ritual of the Bacabs*, though often enigmatic, provides a crucial bridge between scattered sources of pre-Hispanic practices and ethnographic accounts of Yucatec Maya birth rites today. Although previously not always recognized as such, several chants of the *Ritual of the Bacabs* were used for different aspects of Maya perinatal rites during the colonial period. The indigenous Maya medical tradition involves ritual chants, herbal decoctions, and physical manipulation of the patient's body, all of which we have been able to identify in the manuscript texts through the mixed methodology we employed. In this article we have established that chants for cooling a steam bath used in perinatal ritual, for difficulty in childbirth, and for rites regarding the disposal of the afterbirth form a unit in the corpus present in the manuscript. We also elucidated the important role that culture-specific notions of the body, in particular the force called kinam, played in these perinatal rites. We established that ethnographic interviews in present-day Maya communities can aid in these colonial chants' interpretation, yet at the same time these chants invoke deities and accoutrements from the pre-Hispanic era that contemporary Maya healers of today are largely unaware of. As such, no single method of analysis is sufficient in the case of a colonial manuscript as notoriously difficult to interpret as the *Ritual of the Bacabs*. Although the use of indigenous consultants to aid in the translation of colonial manuscripts (Tedlock 1996) and the ethnohistoric reconstruction of elements of Maya medicine (Kunow 2003) is not new, we believe the combination of key consultant interviews, free list interviews, and systematic methods of text analysis (Bernard and Ryan 2010) to be an especially productive methodology. In the present case, this methodology has enriched our knowledge of those rites meant to manage the dangers accompanying colonial Yucatec Maya women's experiences of pregnancy and childbirth. However, such mixed methodologies might be applied productively to other domains where serious impediments exist for the ethnohistoric interpretation of the surviving documentary record.

## Notes

1  We use the colonial orthography for Maya terms throughout this paper in order to maintain fidelity to the original sources as well as to facilitate comparison of this colonial material across epigraphic and ethnographic sources:

b voiced, glottalized bilabial stop
ʦ voiceless, plain alveolar affricate
ɔ voiceless, glottalized alveolar affricate
ch voiceless, plain alveo-palatal affricate
cħ voiceless, glottalized alveo-palatal affricate
h voiceless, laryngeal spirant
j voiceless, velar spirant
c voiceless, plain velar stop
k voiceless, glottalized velar stop
l voiced, alveolar lateral
m voiced, bilabial nasal
n voiced, alveolar nasal
p voiceless, plain bilabial stop
p̱ voiceless, glottalized bilabial stop
z/s voiceless, alveolar fricative

x voiceless, alveo-palatal fricative
t voiceless, plain alveolar stop
tħ voiceless, glottalized alveolar stop
u/v voiced, labiovelar glide
y voiced, palatal glide
a low, central, unrounded vowel
e low, front, unrounded vowel
i/y high, front, unrounded vowel
o low, back, rounded vowel
u high, back, rounded vowel

Phonemic tone is not usually marked in colonial-period Yucatecan alphabetic texts, and therefore is not represented in transcriptions of these texts here. Neither vowel length nor the glottal stop are consistently represented in colonial Yucatecan alphabetic texts either; when a vowel is represented by two letters (*aa*, for example), this may represent either V'V or a long vowel.

2  Dzidz Yam observes in these chants a progression from irrealis to realis language familiar to him from contemporary Maya petitionary speech.

3  Dzidz Yam notes that many of the causes documented ethnographically have to do with bodies' exposure to, or processes involving, *koko kik* ("hot blood").

4  In modern orthography: *k'alal, tóok' yanik beyo'* ("it [the child's head] is trapped, it is *tóok'* like that") (interview, 14 January 2015, Yaxunah, Yucatán, Mexico).

5  Other terms for midwife, such as *x alansah* ("she who facilitates birth") are also used in modern Yucatec.

6  Dzidz Yam has documented similar practices of burning and disposal of the umbilical cord outside the edge of the community in contemporary Quintana Roo during fieldwork in August 2017.

7  There are several examples in the *Ritual of the Bacabs* manuscript of evident confusion by the scribe putting it to writing whether a plain or glottalized consonant was meant by the orator dictating the chants, so either reading is plausible.

8  For analyses of chants where the parts of the hearth are identified explicitly with parts of the god Itzamcab's body, see Knowlton 2015b, 2018.

## References

Analytic Technologies. 2003. *Visual Anthropac version 1.0.1.36. Software for Cultural Domain Analysis: Freelists.* www.analytictech.com.

Anderson, E. N., José Cauich Canul, Aurora Dzib, Salvador Flores Guido, Gerald Ixlebe, Felix Medina Tzuc, Odilón Sánchez Sánchez, and Pastor Valdez Chale. 2003. *Those Who Bring the Flowers: Maya Ethnobotany in Quintana Roo, Mexico.* San Cristóbal de las Casas, Mexico: El Colegio de la Frontera Sur.

Anderson, E. N., and Felix Medina Tzuc. 2005. *Animals and the Maya in Southeast Mexico.* Tucson: University of Arizona Press.

Arzápalo Marín, Ramón. 1987. *El 'Ritual de los Bacabes': Edición facsimilar con transcripción rítmica, traducción, notas, índice, glosario y cómputos estadísticos.* Mexico City: Universidad Nacional Autónoma de México.

Berlo, Janet Catherine. 1983. "The Warrior and the Butterfly: Central Mexican Ideologies of Sacred Warfare and Teotihuacan Iconography." In *Text and Image in Pre-Columbian Art: Essays on the Interrelationship of the Verbal and Visual Arts*, edited by Janet Catherine Berlo, 79–117. Oxford, UK: B.A.R.

Bernard, H. Russell, and Gery W. Ryan. 2010. *Analyzing Qualitative Data: Systematic Approaches*. Thousand Oaks, CA: Sage.

Bricker, Victoria, Eleuterio Po'ot Yah, and Ofelia Dzul de Po'ot. 1998. *A Dictionary of the Maya Language as Spoken in Hocabá, Yucatán*. Salt Lake City: University of Utah Press.

Bricker, Victoria R., and Helga-Maria Miram. 2002. *An Encounter of Two Worlds: The 'Book of Chilam Balam' of Kaua*. Middle American Research Institute, Publication No. 68. New Orleans: Tulane University.

Bruhns, Karen Olsen, and Karen E. Stothert. 2014. *Women in Ancient America*. 2nd ed. Norman: University of Oklahoma Press.

Ciudad Real, Antonio de (attributed). 2001. *Calepino Maya de Motul*, edited by René Acuña. Mexico City: Plaza y Valdes.

Christenson, Allen. 2007. *Popol Vuh: The Sacred Book of the Maya*. Norman: University of Oklahoma Press.

Christenson, Allen. 2008. *Popol Vuh: Literal Poetic Version*. Norman: University of Oklahoma Press.

Chuchiak IV, John F. 2007. "The Sins of the Fathers: Franciscan Friars, Parish Priests, and the Sexual Conquest of the Yucatec Maya, 1545–1808." *Ethnohistory* 54, no.1: 69–127.

Faust, Betty Bernice. 1998. "Cacao Beans and Chili Peppers: Gender Socialization in the Cosmology of a Yucatec Maya Curing Ceremony." *Sex Roles* 39, nos. 7–8: 603–42.

Groark, Kevin P. 1997. "To Warm the Blood, to Warm the Flesh: The Role of the Steambath in Highland Maya (Tzeltal-Tzotzil) Ethnomedicine." *Journal of Latin American Lore* 20, no. 1: 3–96.

Gubler, Ruth. 2018. *Yerbas y hechicerías del Yucatán. Edición, transcripción, traducción y notas*. Mexico City: Universidad Nacional Autónoma de México.

Güémez Pineda, Miguel. 2000. "La concepción del cuerpo humano, la maternidad y el dolor entre mujeres Mayas Yukatekas." *Mesoamérica* 39: 305–32.

Güémez Pineda, Miguel, Patricia Quattrocchi, Feliciano Sánchez Chan, and Erica Barbiani. n.d. Exposición fotográfica: La casa y la cura: Las experiencias de las parteras de Kaua. Universidad Autónoma de Yucatán. www.mayas.uady.mx /exposiciones/exp11.html (accessed 6 November 2018).

Houston, Stephen D. 1996. "Symbolic Sweatbaths of the Maya: Architectural Meaning in the Cross Group at Palenque, Mexico." *Latin American Antiquity* 7, no.2: 132–51.

Houston, Stephen D., Claudia Brittenham, Cassandra Messick, Alexandre Tokovinine, and Christina Warinner. 2009. *Veiled Brightness: A History of Ancient Maya Color*. Austin: University of Texas Press.

Houston, Stephen D., David Stuart, and Karl Taube. 2006. *The Memory of Bones: Body, Being, and Experience among the Classic Maya*. Austin: University of Texas Press.

Jordan, Brigitte. 1993. *Birth in Four Cultures: A Crosscultural Investigation of Childbirth in Yucatan, Holland, Sweden, and the United States*. 4th ed. Long Grove, Il: Waveland Press.

Kellogg, Susan. 2005. *Weaving the Past: A History of Latin America's Indigenous Women from the Prehispanic Period to the Present.* Oxford, UK: Oxford University Press.

Knowlton, Timothy W. 2010. *Maya Creation Myths: Words and Worlds of the "Chilam Balam."* Boulder: University Press of Colorado.

Knowlton, Timothy W. 2012. "Some Historical Continuities in Lowland Maya Magical Speech Genres: Keying Shamanic Performance." In *Parallel Worlds: Genre, Discourse, and Poetics in Contemporary, Colonial, and Classic Maya Literature,* edited by Kerry Hull and Michael D. Carrasco, 253–69. Boulder: University Press of Colorado.

Knowlton, Timothy W. 2015a. "The Maya Goddess of Painting, Writing, and Decorated Textiles." *PARI Journal* 16, no. 2: 31–41.

Knowlton, Timothy W. 2015b. "Literacy and Healing: Semiotic Ideologies and the Entextualization of Colonial Maya Incantations." *Ethnohistory* 62, no. 3: 573–95.

Knowlton, Timothy W. 2016. "Filth and Healing in Yucatan: Interpreting *Ix Hun Ahau,* a Maya Goddess." *Ancient Mesoamerica* 27, no. 2: 319–32.

Knowlton, Timothy W. 2018. "Flame, Icons, and Healing: A Colonial Maya Ontology." *Colonial Latin American Review* 28, no. 3: 392–412.

Kufer, Johanna, and Cameron L. McNeil. 2006. "The Jaguar Tree (*Theobroma bicolor* Bonpl.)." In *Chocolate in Mesoamerica: A Cultural History of Cacao,* edited by Cameron L. McNeil, 90–104. Gainesville: University Press of Florida.

Kunow, Marianna Appel. 2003. *Maya Medicine: Traditional Healing in Yucatán.* Albuquerque: University of New Mexico Press.

Landa, Diego de. (ca. 1566) 1978. *Yucatan before and after the Conquest,* translated by William Gates. New York: Dover.

Lévi-Strauss, Claude. 1950. "The Effectiveness of Symbols." In *Structural Anthropology,* translated by Claire Jacobson and Brooke Grundfest Schoepf, 186–205. New York: Basic.

Love, Bruce. 2012. *Maya Shamanism Today: Connecting with the Cosmos in Rural Yucatan.* San Francisco: Precolumbia Mesoweb Press.

Martínez Huchim, Ana Patricia. 2006. *Diccionario Maya: Español-Maya, Maya-Español.* Mérida, Mexico: Dante.

Miram, Helga-Maria, and Wolfgang Miram. 1988. *Concordance of the 'Chilam Balames'.* 6 vols. Hamburg: Toro.

Polanco, Edward Anthony. 2018. "'I Am Just a Tiçitl': Decolonizing Central Mexican Nahua Female Healers, 1535–1635." *Ethnohistory* 65, no.3: 441–63.

Pretchel, Martin, and Robert S. Carlsen. 1988. "Weaving and Cosmos amongst the Tzutujil Maya of Guatemala." *Res: Anthropology and Aesthetics* 15: 122–32.

Quinlan, Marsha. 2005. "Considerations for Collecting Freelists in the Field: Examples from Ethnobotany." *Field Methods* 17, no. 3: 219–34.

Redfield, Robert, and Margaret Park Redfield. 1940. "Disease and Its Treatment in Dzitas, Yucatan." In *Contributions to American Anthropology and History, Volume 6, No. 30–34.* Washington, DC: Carnegie Institution of Washington.

Redfield, Robert, and Alfonso Villa Rojas. 1934. *Chan Kom: A Maya Village.* Carnegie Institution of Washington, Publication No. 448. Washington, DC: Judd and Detweiler.

Restall, Matthew. 1995. "'He Wished It in Vain': Subordination and Resistance among Maya Women in Post-Conquest Yucatan." *Ethnohistory* 42, no.4: 577–94.

Restall, Matthew. 2003. "A History of the New Philology and the New Philology in History." *Latin American Research Review* 38, no. 1: 113–34.

*Ritual of the Bacabs.* ca. 1779. Garret-Gates Manuscripts no. 1. Princeton University Library. pudl.princeton.edu/objects/bn999802r (accessed 15 January 2018).

Rodríguez Angulo, Elsa María, María Guadalupe Andueza-Pech, and Yolanda Oliva Peña. 2018. "Characteristics of Maternal Death among Mayan Women in Yucatan, Mexico." In *Maternal Death and Pregnancy-Related Morbidity among Indigenous Women in Mexico and Central America: An Anthropological, Epidemiological, and Biomedical Approach*, edited by David A. Schwartz, 249–70. Cham, Switzerland: Springer.

Roys, Ralph L. 1931. *The Ethno-Botany of the Maya.* Middle American Research Institute, Publication No. 2. New Orleans: Tulane University.

Roys, Ralph L. 1933. *The "Book of Chilam Balam" of Chumayel.* Carnegie Institution of Washington, Publication No. 438. Washington, DC: W. F. Roberts.

Roys, Ralph L. 1965. *Ritual of the Bacabs.* Norman: University of Oklahoma Press.

Schwartz, David A. 2018a. "Aztec Pregnancy: Archaeological and Cultural Foundations for Motherhood and Childbearing in Ancient Mesoamerica." In *Maternal Death and Pregnancy-Related Morbidity among Indigenous Women in Mexico and Central America: An Anthropological, Epidemiological, and Biomedical Approach*, edited by David A. Schwartz, 11–33. Cham, Switzerland: Springer.

Schwartz, David A. 2018b. "Hypertensive Mothers, Obstetric Hemorrhage, and Infections: Biomedical Aspects of Maternal Death Among Indigenous Women in Mexico and Central America." In *Maternal Death and Pregnancy-Related Morbidity among Indigenous Women in Mexico and Central America: An Anthropological, Epidemiological, and Biomedical Approach*, edited by David A. Schwartz, 35–50. Cham, Switzerland: Springer.

Sesia, Paola. 2016. "Maternal Death in Mexico." In *Oxford Research Encyclopedia, Latin American History.* Oxford: Oxford University Press. oxfordre.com/latinamericanhistory/.

Socolow, Susan Migden. 2015. *The Women of Colonial Latin America.* 2nd ed. New York: Cambridge University Press.

Sullivan, Thelma D. 1982. "Tlazolteotl-Ixcuina: The Great Spinner and Weaver. In *The Art and Iconography of Late Post-Classic Central Mexico*, edited by Elizabeth Hill Boone, 7–35. Washington, DC: Dumbarton Oaks.

Sullivan, Thelma D., and Timothy J. Knab. 1994. *A Scattering of Jades: Stories, Poems, and Prayers of the Aztecs.* New York: Simon and Schuster.

Taube, Karl A. 1994. "The Birth Vase: Natal Imagery in Ancient Maya Myth and Ritual." In *The Maya Vase Book, Volume 4*, edited by Justin Kerr. New York: Justin Kerr.

Taube, Karl A. 1998. "The Jade Hearth: Centrality, Rulership, and the Classic Maya Temple." In *Function and Meaning in Classic Maya Architecture*, edited by Stephen D. Houston, 427–69. Washington, DC: Dumbarton Oaks.

Taube, Karl A. 2001. "Butterflies." In *The Oxford Encyclopedia of Mesoamerican Cultures, Volume 1*, edited by David Carrasco, 107–09. Oxford: Oxford University Press.

Tedlock, Dennis. 1996. *Popol Vuh: The Mayan Book of the Dawn of Life*. Rev ed. New York: Simon and Schuster.

Thompson, J. Eric S. 1970. *Maya History and Religion*. Norman: University of Oklahoma Press.

Vail, Gabrielle, and Andrea Stone. 2002. "Representations of Women in Postclassic and Colonial Maya Literature and Art." In *Ancient Maya Women*, edited by Traci Ardren, 203–28. Walnut Creek, CA: Altamira Press.

Veile, Amanda, and Karen L. Kramer. 2018. "Pregnancy, Birth, and Babies: Motherhood and Modernization in a Yucatec Village." In *Maternal Death and Pregnancy-Related Morbidity among Indigenous Women in Mexico and Central America: An Anthropological, Epidemiological, and Biomedical Approach*, edited by David A. Schwartz, 205–23. Cham, Switzerland: Springer.

Villa Rojas, Alfonso. 1945. *The Maya of East Central Quintana Roo*. Carnegie Institution of Washington, Publication No. 559. Baltimore: Lord Baltimore Press.

Villa Rojas, Alfonso. 1980. "La imagen del cuerpo humano según los Mayas de Yucatán." *Anales de Antropologia* 17, no. 2: 31–46.

# Book Reviews

The Motions Beneath: Indigenous Migrants of the Urban Frontier of New Spain. By Laurent Corbeil. (Tucson: The University of Arizona Press, 2018. xi+273 pp., acknowledgements, introduction, maps, appendix, glossary, bibliography, index. $55.00 cloth.)

Susan M. Deeds, *Northern Arizona University*

In this well-researched book, Laurent Corbeil offers the story of how a complex mix of indigenous migrants from central areas of Mexico moved beneath the structures of colonialism and actively contributed to the creation of a flourishing economy and society during the first forty years of the city of San Luis Potosí. In sorting out these multiethnic northward migrations, concepts of mobility and identity thread through his analysis.

How does this study fit into a larger narrative that has highlighted the migrations of many thousands of indigenous peoples to New Spain's northern frontiers from the sixteenth century onward? To date, the two most documented patterns of this migration involve *indios conquistadores*, who accompanied early Spanish expeditions and homogenous Tlaxcalan "colonies," financed by the crown to assist Spaniards in acculturating the north's mostly nonsedentary natives. A third pattern concerns the migrants who filled the labor demands of the silver mining economy that evolved in sparsely populated areas. Although this manifestation of heterogeneous migration was actually the most massive in terms of overall numbers, it has only recently begun to be studied in its enormous complexity. For example, in *Urban Indians in a Silver City: Zacatecas, Mexico, 1546–1806* (2016),

*Ethnohistory* 66:4 (October 2019)   DOI 10.1215/00141801-7683330
Copyright 2019 by American Society for Ethnohistory

Dana Velasco Murillo examines multiethnic migrants to New Spain's primary silver city over the *longue durée*, demonstrating how they shaped semi-autonomous communities by adapting Spanish institutions like the *cofradía* to protect their interests.

Focusing on a shorter time span, Corbeil also addresses the more substantial and relatively neglected history of labor migration by detailing how multiethnic indigenous migrants re-created communities and identities in San Luis Potosí. Although an organized contingent of Tlaxcalans arrived there in 1591 to help incorporate local Guachichils, Corbeil shows that this type of corporate migration, in which ethnicity was the primary marker of identity, was atypical in San Luis Potosí. Many other factors, most especially mobility, influenced how indigenous people created affiliations and identified themselves. They arrived primarily as individuals or in small groups from over a hundred communities of origin and included Tarascans, Nahuas, Otomis, Cocas, Tecuexes, and Cazcans among others. In many cases they had made stops along the way, through a variety of landscapes, contacts, and languages.

In San Luis Potosí itself, indigenous people interacted across a conurbation, or tight networks of distinct, yet interdependent communities. Drawing on a painstaking reading of a variety of sources, including local parish and criminal records, Corbeil shows how mobility across worksites where labor teams were not ethnically homogeneous facilitated contacts and economic ties that gave individuals multiple affiliations. Daily encounters in drinking establishments, commercial activities, and craft production also encouraged interethnic relations. Catholic marriage and baptism created extended family bonds. Contacts could also foment enmities that played out in drunken brawls and other violence. After the first twenty years, even as newcomers continued to arrive, the children of migrants constituted a core population that was consolidating indigenous social structures and hierarchies. Formerly loosely organized pueblos and *barrios de indios* developed official discourses and corporate identities to defend themselves against Spaniards, as competition for land increased. These corporate identities were based more on living spaces than origin or ethnicity and, according to Corbeil, contributed to creating some stability in the transition from mining to other productive economic activities.

A study that goes beyond the early years will no doubt reveal other structures and changes in social organization as well as specifically gendered contributions to the developing conurbation. Nonetheless, this microcosmic reading of the early socially heterogeneous, disorderly past of San Luis Potosí is filled with individual stories and insights that demonstrate the

complexity of social relations and individual affiliations among indigenous peoples who were dynamically involved in creating a productive and
flourishing economy and society, however socially differentiated. The book
adds significantly to a trend that addresses gaps in our understanding of
how Mesoamericans influenced the development of New Spain's north.

Sustaining the Divine in Mexico Tenochtitlan: Nahuas and Catholicism,
1523–1700. By Jonathan Truitt. (Norman: University of Oklahoma Press,
2018. xiv +281 pp., acknowledgements, introduction, maps, illustrations,
images, bibliography, appendix, index. $45.00 cloth.)

William F. Connell, *Christopher Newport University*

Jonathan Truitt, in this book, *Sustaining the Divine in Mexico Tenochtitlan*,
engages how Nahuas and other indigenous peoples in Mexico Tenochtitlan
came to support and use Catholicism and the institutions of the Catholic
Church under colonialism. Truitt begins his fifth chapter with a clear and
direct statement of the book's argument—he wrote that although Spaniards introduced Catholicism, "it was the Mesoamericans themselves who
proved crucial to fostering the faith" (191). Placed in the context of a
chapter that discusses the native artisanal production, Truitt reveals the
eloquence and significance of his argument—Nahuas and other Mesoamerican peoples thirsted for the spiritual apparatus, community, and ave-
nues for position of stature and authority provided by the Church. They
thus made rational choices to embrace Catholicism because it served their
interests.

　　Many who have studied the interactions between Nahuas and Euro-
peans after the Spanish invasion have focused on Nahua resistance to or
misunderstanding of European religion. Others have focused on the preservation of independent native identity depicting elements of resistance to
European colonialism. Truitt, however, does not return to the heroic narrative of Robert Ricard, who overstated and mischaracterized the "successful" inculcation of the native peoples. Rather, the argument builds on
the work of historians, ethnohistorians, and anthropologists who have
added nuance to that institutional story to show that Nahuas found in
Catholicism the rituals, community, and spirituality that they desired.

　　The book is thematically organized and situated temporally in the
mid-sixteenth through seventeenth centuries. Thematic chapters focus on
religious space, evangelization, gender, *cofradías* (religious brotherhoods),
and indigenous production of religious goods. The work relies on a broad
reading of the viceregal evidence in both Spanish and Nahuatl. Material
comes from archives in Europe and Mexico and also North American
library collections. The work has brought to the attention of scholars new
Nahuatl documents previously undiscovered, including sixty wills. Truitt's

*Ethnohistory* 66:4 (October 2019)　DOI 10.1215/00141801-7683348
Copyright 2019 by American Society for Ethnohistory

clear discussions of historiography old and new and his careful reading of Spanish and Nahuatl sources make this a compelling contribution to the history of evangelization, but also to the history of indigenous Mexico City. Even though the focus stays consistently on Nahuas and Catholicism, the book relates that these themes cannot be separated from a broader discussion of the Nahua experience in the city.

Readers will find novel themes among the many topics discussed. The book includes a lengthy discussion of music to show how Nahuas, who had their own musical traditions, embraced European musical styles and instruments. The Spanish loan word, *trompeta*, for example, entered Nahuatl as early as 1551, demonstrating that no comparable instrument existed in native society before its introduction, but also that Nahuas rapidly incorporated its use into writings in their language as they did with other nouns for which they had no equivalent and which were ubiquitous or important to them. Furthermore, by focusing on everyday Nahuas and their interactions with the Church, through cofradías, participation in community activities, and through music, art, and artisanal production, the book highlights the ordinary experiences of native peoples that so rarely emerges from colonial histories.

Truitt has also included many features that ethnohistorians will find particularly useful. The book includes an appendix with documents in Nahuatl and translated into English. Scholars will also appreciate the tables, which provide exact locations and descriptions of all indigenous wills he encountered, ranging temporally from 1546 to 1725, and other helpful guides for locating documents used in the book. Finally, it is richly illustrated with maps, photographs of documents, sheet music, and codex images.

Overall, Truitt has contributed a major work in the study of indigenous Mexico Tenochtitlan. His focus on the Church, built on the work of other scholars of Nahua evangelization, helps to explain native spirituality under colonialism. In so doing, Truitt also helps to explain the development of indigenous society, particularly the urban milieu, as it became increasingly diverse through the in migration of various groups during the beginning of the eighteenth century.

**Slavery and Utopia: The Wars and Dreams of an Amazonian World Transformer.** By Fernando Santos-Granero. (Austin: University of Texas Press, 2018. 285 pp., contents, illustrations, acknowledgments, prologue, epilogue, glossary, notes, references, index. $29.95 paperback.)

**The Rise and Fall of the Amazon Rubber Industry: An Historical Anthropology.** By Stephen L. Nugent. (New York: Routledge, 2018. 207 pp., contents, list of illustrations, preface, acknowledgements, references, index. $44.95 paper.)

Robert Wasserstrom, *Terra Group*

In 1915 an Indigenous leader named Juan Carlos Tasorentsi and several thousand followers laid waste to rubber estates across a large swathe of Peru's Selva Central rainforest. Conservative journalists quickly defaulted to the civilization-versus-barbarism trope, but other writers were not so sure. For the previous at least twenty years, they noted, rubber barons had moved deep into the Peruvian Amazon. At first, many native groups had been willing to work in exchange for tools, cloth, and other useful things. They stopped producing their own food and added it to the bill. Later, as the supply of "willing" debt peons dried up, estate owners turned to slavery. Often, they outsourced this trade to local chieftains, whose raids (*correrías*) terrorized native people over a vast hinterland.

And then disaster struck. After 1910 plantation rubber from Southeast Asia began pouring onto the world market. The price of Amazonian *jebe* plummeted and useful things—including food—became much harder to get. Indigenous peons felt cheated and betrayed. In 1913 and 1914, they drove whites and mestizos out of the Pichis basin. Tasorentsi's uprising broke out a few months later.

No one knows more about the Peruvian rubber boom than Fernando Santos-Granero. His 1999 book *Tamed Frontiers: Economy, Society, and Civil Rights In Upper Amazonia* (written with Frederica Barclay) should be on everybody's reading list. In *Slavery and Utopia*, he tells this complex story through the remarkable life of Tasorentsi, Ashaninka chief. Born in 1875, Tasorentsi (whose name he translates as "world transformer") had worked first as a debt peon and then moved on to slave trading. Later, according to Santos-Granero, he underwent a moral awakening. Rejecting slavery, he set out to "remove white people from the region through a combination of guerrilla tactics and shamanic warfare" (108). In the early

*Ethnohistory* 66:4 (October 2019)   DOI 10.1215/00141801-7683366
Copyright 2019 by American Society for Ethnohistory

1920s, Tasorentsi's life took another remarkable turn: he converted to Seventh Day Adventism, especially its belief that the end times were close at hand. To him, this meant that Indigenous people would soon live without white enslavers again. He died in 1958, rejected by an Adventist church that had become more orthodox.

In reconstructing Tasorentsi's dramatic story, Santos-Granero promises a new "historical anthropology, a hybrid book combining the conventions of anthropology and history . . . that differs substantially in both style and methodology from other historical works on Lowland South America" (5). The result is only partly successful. While rubber collection was still a living memory, very few researchers recorded the kind of systematic oral histories that would have provided richer sources. Inevitably, key episodes in Tasorentsi's life—as a debt peon, slave raider, and emerging prophet—remain shrouded in conjecture and hearsay.

To cover the gaps, Santos-Granero often falls back on ethnographic extrapolation or wishful thinking. For example, no contemporary sources connect Tasorentsi to the 1913–14 precursor rebellion. Yet Santos-Granero insists that he must have played a central role, perhaps even greater than its acknowledged leader. Why? Because "the fact that both men lived in the same general area . . . seems to be more than a mere coincidence" (84). Maybe so, maybe not. Here and elsewhere, Santos-Granero might have usefully stuck closer to the conventions of history. To my mind, Blanca Muratorio's *The Life and Times of Grandfather Alonso: Culture and History in the Upper Amazon* (originally published in 1987) remains the touchstone for historical anthropology in western Amazonia, although Santos-Granero unjustly dismisses it as old school.

Focusing on Brazil, in *The Rise and Fall of the Amazon Rubber Industry* Stephen L. Nugent pursues a very different objective. "This is not a history of the rubber industry in the Amazon," he explains, "but an essay about the writing of that history—not historiography, but, for want of a better term, historical anthropology" (3). In his view, academic and other accounts of the Amazonian rubber boom have generally perpetuated a stereotype of failed economic growth, a "still-to-be-integrated realm of raw materials" that resists modernity. "The customary overreliance on the boom designation serves to mask complex, historical social landscapes in Amazonia past and present, and helps to sustain the idea of a permanent frontier region whose only possible destiny is as a source of what is obsessively portrayed as *natural wealth*" (5–6). He also points to "Anthropological Amazonia," where "the default assumption has long been . . . that contemporary [Indigenous] societies are significantly representative of their prehistoric antecedents" (43). Invoking Sidney Mintz's *Sweetness and Power*

(1985), he suggests alternatively that "reconstituted peasantries" there are the outcome of capitalist expansion, not its absence.

Most of Nugent's book explores the commodity chain that has linked Amazonia to manufacturing in the US and Great Britain. Worldwide commodity production took place unevenly, he reminds us, but it transformed everything in its path. Nothing was ever the same again. Anyone who suggests that the Amazon or Highland New Guinea or other provinces of the anthropological imaginary escaped its impact faces a heavy burden of proof.

Yet Nugent's arguments also have a musty feel. Since the 1990s, few serious researchers would claim that Amazonia represents an anachronistic, out-of-date backwater. That conceit now belongs almost exclusively to tourism operators, feature writers, and development agencies, whose self-interest lies in marketing primitiveness. And while Mintz's work certainly opened a door for anthropologists, Nugent might have benefited from more recent commodity history: Sven Beckert's magnificent *Empire of Cotton: A Global History* (2014) comes to mind. On a smaller scale, most readers will probably be unconvinced by his overthinking of the term *rubber boom*. Generally speaking, it refers to a specific period of wild rubber production (roughly 1870–1910 in Brazil; 1885–1930 upriver toward the Andes), not a stereotype of long-term economic failure. Still, for readers who want to make the connection between factories in London and rubber *estradas* in Brazil, he provides a great deal of useful information.

**Frontiers of Citizenship: A Black and Indigenous History of Postcolonial Brazil.** By Yuko Miki. (Cambridge: Cambridge University Press, 2018. xix +292 pp., introduction, map, bibliography, index. £75.00 cloth.)

James P. Woodard, *Montclair State University*

A decade ago the distinguished historian of Brazil Barbara Weinstein challenged Latin Americanists to "combine the 'Indo' and the 'Afro'" in studies of the region's postcolonial history. Yuko Miki's *Frontiers of Citizenship*, though not initially conceived in response to that challenge, represents an endorsement of Weinstein's program, as well as a major accomplishment for its author. Readers of *Ethnohistory* will find much to admire in its charting of the complex intersections of indigenous and diasporic peoples over the course of nineteenth-century Brazilian history, from early experiments in nation building through the aftermath of the abolition of slavery in its last New World redoubt, in 1888.

The impact of these intersecting histories, Miki argues, echoed through the length of the continent-sized country into the twentieth century and on to our time, but their site — the site of the particular histories she documents — was much more limited. It consisted of what she calls the "Atlantic Frontier," a Brazilian region south of the most successful experiments in colonial sugar-plantation agriculture, east of the mining zone that boomed for much of the eighteenth century, and north of Rio de Janeiro, the colonial and later national capital, and its growing plantation hinterland. This region remained largely uncolonized until the nineteenth century, and so, under the canopy of unspoiled Atlantic forest, at the jurisdictional intersection of three territorial units (after independence, in 1822, the provinces of Bahia, Minas Gerais, and Espírito Santo) were potentially rich lands to be exploited for the benefit of nation, settler, and state. The lands, though uncolonized, were not empty of human inhabitants, but rather were a haven to autonomous indigenous peoples, who would have to be dealt with in some way or another were the lands to be settled by Brazilians and by European immigrants. At the same time, in nineteenth-century Brazilian terms at least, effective settlement and exploitation meant the expansion of the country's most genuinely national institution, chattel slavery, however much some statesmen might have wished otherwise.

And so the stage was set for the stories Miki tells so well, over six chapters, drawing on multiple archives and an array of published sources.

*Ethnohistory* 66:4 (October 2019)   DOI 10.1215/00141801-7683384
Copyright 2019 by American Society for Ethnohistory

Her first chapter explains how the settlement of the Atlantic Frontier and its incorporation into effectively national territory produced patterns of exclusion and exploitation, including the introduction of large numbers of African slaves alongside the renewal, on fresh ground, of Indian slavery, as the people outsiders called Botocudo were subject to "just war" (from 1808) and legal enslavement (until 1831), while the traffic in native peoples, especially children, continued for decades thereafter. Chapter 2 explores black and indigenous struggles for—variously—freedom, autonomy, and inclusion in and around the Atlantic Frontier, while chapter 3 steps back, charting how a nineteenth-century "extinction discourse" regarding native peoples took shape at the national level—according to which the Botocudo and kindred groups were fast becoming extinct—and how this discourse prefigured subsequent discourses regarding the anticipated disappearance of "blacks" from Brazil, an interesting connection unacknowledged in the considerable literature on Brazilian racial thought. The three remaining chapters return to the Atlantic Frontier, with some elapsed time in the interim: the focus is now on the 1870s and especially the 1880s, as the slow ending of Brazilian slavery heightened local tensions, even as manifestations of these tensions (differential treatment of anti-indigenous and antiblack crime, slave appropriation of local geography, increased settler interest in indigenous labor, and different kinds of abolitionism) are taken to be characteristic of larger struggles over nationhood, territory, and citizenship. An epilogue offers an explication of the project's origins (it was inspired by archival findings rather than in direct response to Weinstein's challenge, though Weinstein was a mentor to the author, and the published version of her call is cited in the notes, as it could not but be).

Summary scarcely does justice to such a fine first book, which will be of great interest to historians of slavery, frontier settlement, and the native peoples of the Americas, as well as historians of Brazil generally. Some readers will find that the idea of citizenship scarcely bears the load it is asked to carry, as an underexamined organizing conceit stretched through chapters that stand up on their own, but that is little matter. Miki's carefully told stories of the intersections of black and indigenous experiences across a formative period in the history of the largest of Latin American countries, the historical meaning of these stories, and their potential conceptual impact are what make this book so worthwhile.

Our Beloved Kin: A New History of King Philip's War. By Lisa Brooks.
(New Haven, CT: Yale University Press, 2018. xv +431 pp., maps, acknowledgments, notes, index. $35.00 cloth.)

Jon Parmenter, *Cornell University*

To elicit the Indigenous point of view from unforgiving sources has represented a key goal of ethnohistorical scholarship for more than sixty years.
Lisa Brooks's inspiring new account of King Philip's War marks a signal
accomplishment of that objective. One might wonder what could be left to
say about this much-studied conflict, but Brooks demonstrates that a return
to overlooked primary documents, an emphasis on previously neglected
personalities, and detailed reconstructions of events-as-lived, all informed
by a deep understanding of Indigenous "strategies and logics" (187), can
tell us much of value that is new.

Centering her narrative on the life stories of Wampanoag *saunskwa*
(female hereditary leader) Weetamoo and the Nipmuc scholar James Printer,
Brooks offers dramatic new insights into Native peoples' complex moti-
vations for resistance to settler intrusions in 1675, as well as the alliances
they constructed to maintain their independence and minimize the impact
of the war on their communities and families. No account of the war to date
has explained the Native side of the story in a manner as convincing or
compelling as Brooks has accomplished.

Brooks employs the stories of Weetamoo and James Printer to illus-
trate, respectively, two key themes of seventeenth-century Northeastern
Algonquian ethnohistory: the "deed game," by which New England settlers
employed increasingly complex and egregious fraud to separate Native
people from their land, and the tensions caused by conversions to Christianity in Native communities. Brooks then weaves together these narrative threads to provide a groundbreaking interpretation of the war's origins
and its impact on various Native populations.

Careful readings of colonial documents represent the heart of Brooks's
approach—her recovery of Weetamoo, the sister of Metacom's (i.e., "King
Philip's") wife, offers an instructive lesson in how historians and leaders
will profit from a willingness to re-read documentary evidence against the
grain of its authors' assumptions of gender norms. The book's painstaking reconstruction of the war's origins reframes our understanding of the
choices made by Metacom and his kin in June 1675 as a targeted assault on

*Ethnohistory* 66:4 (October 2019)   DOI 10.1215/00141801-7683402
Copyright 2019 by American Society for Ethnohistory

specific aggressors. Brooks challenges colonial narratives of the war's key events with skilled assessments of the sources. She recasts traditional interpretations of the Wampanoags' August 1675 "siege" of Brookfield as a failed effort to inflict mass casualties on the settler population, highlighting how the "siege" actually represented an attempt by the Wampanoags to reclaim illegally taken land by eliminating markers of settler occupancy (such as structures and livestock) and intimidating settlers into leaving. This is not mere semantic nuance. Brooks demonstrates repeatedly that the basis for many of the decisions made by the "hostile" Wampanoag, Narragansett, and Nipmuc nations during King Philip's War derived from a comprehensible context of rational self-interest vis-à-vis settler transgressions.

Brooks ensures that her readers understand just how much of King Philip's War revolved around the question of freedom of movement for Indigenous peoples. While Weetamoo and Metacom leveraged their capacity for secure mobility through Indigenous homelands to pursue resistance, New England colonists redefined "Indians" into a single racial category that they sought to contain and control—the latter phenomenon demonstrated most clearly in the case of the "Praying Indians," whose fate Brooks illustrates through her account of James Printer.

By exploring alternatives to the "replacement narratives," which end histories of the war with Metacom's death, Brooks shows us a way out of the trap of dismissing Indigenous resistance as an exercise in futility. This is a remarkable book that should be read by all who aspire to understand colonial American history.

Captain Cook's Final Voyage: The Untold Story from the Journals of James Burney and Henry Roberts. Edited by James K. Barnett. (Pullman: Washington State University Press, 2017. xvii+323 pp., preface, foreword, introduction, illustrations, notes, bibliography, index. $34.95 paper.)

David Igler, *University of California, Irvine*

The published journals of Captain James Cook comprise the core of the canon for scholars of oceanic exploration, especially as it pertains to the Pacific Ocean in the late eighteenth and early nineteenth centuries. Cook's successors, including George Vancouver, Alejandro Malaspina, and Adam Johann von Krusenstern, among countless others, also utilized his journals as their guidebooks for not only all matters geographic and oceanographic, but also for proper behavior and protocol when dealing with officers, crew, and indigenous communities. The great editor J. C. Beaglehole expanded the Cook journals in size and significance by including references to (and corroborating data from) the many journals of Cook's officers and companions, such as the naturalist Joseph Banks and the officer Charles Clerke. Some journals of the third and final Cook voyage were never published, including those authored by Henry Roberts and James Burney, which are now partially available thanks to James K. Barnett's *Captain Cook's Final Voyage: The Untold Story from the Journals of James Burney and Henry Roberts*.

Henry Roberts, only nineteen years old when he took ship on the HMS *Resolution* (the companion ship to Cook's HMS *Discovery*), served as a master's mate throughout the voyage, which embarked to search for a passage (the Northwest Passage) and sailed well north of the Bering Strait. Along the way Cook had the good fortune to encounter (some say "discover") the Hawai'ian Islands in 1778 and the less good fortune when he returned the following year, after the British visitors had worn out their welcome there, before he was killed at Kealakekua Bay. Roberts witnessed—or at least was present for—all the major events of this historic expedition. Also present was James Burney, who sailed on Cook's previous voyage and served as a second officer to Charles Clerke, who died of tuberculosis some months after Cook's demise. Together, their journals cast additional light on what scholars largely know about the third voyage: the officers and sailors were incredibly lucky to survive the daring exploration of the icy far north, Cook's behavior turned increasingly erratic as the

*Ethnohistory* 66:4 (October 2019)   DOI 10.1215/00141801-7683420
Copyright 2019 by American Society for Ethnohistory

voyage progressed, and the culminating events in Hawai'i were tragic in multiple ways, not the least of which was the introduction of venereal diseases to the island population.

Barnett edits these journals superbly. He moves the reader through the various stages of the voyage (the South Seas, the North Pacific, Hawai'i, and back north before the return to England) with carefully edited sections from the journals corresponding to each location. Roberts's perspective from the lower ranks of sailors complements Burney's view from the officer class; for instance, north of Nootka Sound Roberts describes the near death of "one of our seamen" who was dragged under the water by a "boring rope" (146) and nearly drowned, while the following day Burney offered ethnographic observations of the Nuuchahnulth inhabitants' language and facial scarring (137). Both writers seemed acutely aware of their roles as journalist-observers, whether they were describing the condition of Aleuts under the yoke of Russian overseers or the dramatic death of Cook and four marines, who died in the violent confrontation at Kealakekua Bay, of whom Burney bemoaned "their Bodies [were now] in possession of the Indians" (225).

Barnett located these two essentially unknown journals in the State Library of New South Wales, which raises the issue of how much more Cook material is out there, still unpublished. His text is richly illustrated with works by his expedition artist John Webber, in addition to surprisingly skillful drawings completed by Burney and Roberts. In sum, *Captain Cook's Final Voyage* represents a deeply researched and handsomely produced addition to an ever-growing body of literature on Cook's explorations in the Pacific.

Unsettling the West: Violence and State Building in the Ohio Valley. By Rob Harper. (Philadelphia: University of Pennsylvania Press, 2018. xvi +250 pp., abbreviations, acknowledgments, notes, bibliography, index. $45.00 cloth.)

Rebecca Kugel, *University of California, Riverside*

Rob Harper's new work, *Unsettling the West*, is a welcome entry in the literature that examines early modern state building. Focusing on the eighteenth century Ohio Valley, Harper explores the interconnections between violence, state building, and colonialism. American state building in Ohio, Harper argues, challenges both top-down and bottom-up interpretations of the subject, and particularly disputes long-standing assumptions that only minimal violence accompanied American state formation. Classic Weberian models of orderly top-down state formation did not occur, nor was the Ohio Valley a region where individualistic Turnerian settlers, disdaining established political authority, developed a state-building process that was both democratically bottom-up and violence free. Harper emphasizes that the Turnerian interpretation, by skimming lightly over the violence that accompanied what used to be disingenuously termed "American westward movement," missed an important opportunity to analyze the centrality of violence to American state formation, not to mention Native dispossession.

Violence in the Ohio Valley also owed much to the region's long history as contested colonial space. The French and British empires, British settlers from the seaboard colonies, and Shawnees, Delawares, Wyandots, and Haudenosaunees, all jockeyed for control of the region in the seventeenth and early eighteenth centuries. None completely succeeded, making the Ohio Valley a place where multiple representatives of multiple polities sought to exercise power, including British imperial agents and military commanders, Indigenous diplomats and political leaders, and colonial officials ranging from governors and influential legislators to local militia officers and traders. In response, Ohio's tribal nations and settler colonists made selective, opportunistic alliances, with each other as well as among themselves. Through these interethnic and intercultural coalitions and the patronage networks they created, Ohio's inhabitants attempted to manipulate multiple sources of governmental power in pursuit of locally desired objectives. One of their major concerns was containing intercommunity

*Ethnohistory* 66:4 (October 2019) DOI 10.1215/00141801-7683438
Copyright 2019 by American Society for Ethnohistory

violence. Individual mediators or larger coalitions strove, often successfully, to prevent violent encounters between small parties of Native peoples and colonists from spiraling into general warfare.

Engaging with colonial governments was risky business, however. State officials sought to bolster their feeble authority by extending state power into the Ohio country, frequently by force of arms. Government-supplied weapons and soldiers destabilized the painstakingly constructed local coalitions, allowing Native peoples and land-hungry colonists the means to wage renewed war while, in Harper's words, "leaving their respective peoples desperate for state protection" (20). Each outbreak of organized violence drove Ohio Valley residents into closer alliances with emergent state power in an attempt to restrain the violence that state officials (possibly even the same ones now being incorporated into a reconstituted coalition) had unleashed in the first place. The result remained a complex political landscape of negotiation and networking in which Native nations, colonists, and government officials participated in remaking the political order after the collapse of the British colonial system in the 1780s.

A new American "imperial republic" (176) fitfully emerged by the 1790s. Harper emphasizes that both Native peoples and settlers participated in the creation of this state, though with diametrically opposed expectations of their place in it. Harper claims that Native peoples remained a recognized component within the new American polity, an analysis that seems to rely on present-day legal understandings of Native nations as third sovereign spaces. This assessment seems dubious; the immediate reality of the early American state was an unwelcoming one for Native peoples. Settlers would continue forcing Native peoples from the Ohio Valley, by fair means and foul, using the legal mechanism of treaty-based land cessions but also through all-too-familiar acts of violence.

Patrolling the Border: Theft and Violence on the Creek-Georgia Frontier, 1770–1796. By Joshua S. Haynes. (Athens: University of Georgia Press, 2018. xiv +294 pp., maps, illustrations, acknowledgements, notes, bibliography, index. $59.95 cloth.)

Steven J. Peach, *Tarleton State University*

In *Patrolling the Border: Theft and Violence on the Creek-Georgia Frontier, 1770–1796,* Joshua Haynes investigates the motives, methods, and consequences of Creek raids along the Creek-Georgia frontier in the late eighteenth century. Positioning Creek raiders front and center in his narrative, Haynes intervenes in key debates on southern Indian politics, Creek-Georgia relations, and Native American raiding strategies. Drawing on imperial, federal, and state records, he demonstrates that Creek raids are best understood as "border patrols" committed to a "broad political vision of territorial integrity and political sovereignty" (13–14). Anything but "aimless," Creek raids championed Creek sovereignty and "acted in accord with consensus" reached in raiders' towns (13).

The book's eight original chapters track the ebb and flow of Creek raids. Probing damages claims lodged by Georgia settlers, Haynes finds that Creeks executed 977 raids on or near Georgia properties between 1770 and 1800. Creeks stole property more than they killed settlers, however, because most raids ended in theft and only a little more than 150 produced death or injury (90, 111, 135, 171). Moreover, Haynes uses mapping methods to conclude that 76 percent (or 746) of all raids targeted the coveted and contested Oconee River valley lying on the Creeks' border with Georgia (7).

Lower Creeks inaugurated border patrols starting in 1770. They "evicted" settlers and confiscated property from illicit British settlements in West Florida and Georgia (26). Up to 1800, few raids ended in bloodshed. Creeks were less interested in killing white settlers than in protecting land from the newcomers. During the American Revolution, for example, Lower and Upper Creek patrolmen sought to reclaim the controversial New Purchase Cession of 1773. Warriors launched 102 raids on the ceded lands, but only 24 resulted in bloodshed (64). Following a spike in Creek raiding in 1778, violence along the Creek-Georgia frontier diminished.

The 1786 Treaty of Shoulderbone Creek was a "turning point" for Creek raiders, however(105). It confirmed earlier treaties that had ceded

*Ethnohistory* 66:4 (October 2019)   DOI 10.1215/00141801-7683456

the east bank of the Oconee to Georgia and highlighted Georgia's aggressive tactics toward Creek delegates. As a result, Creek raids jumped up "600 percent" between 1787 and 1790 (130). Only in 1796, when Creeks signed the Treaty of Coleraine with the US confirming the Oconee border, did Creeks and Georgians achieve an uneasy truce. Afterward, Creek-Georgia violence "declined steadily" (189). Yet in the period under study, Georgia governors and militia captains rarely acknowledged Creek raiders' political aims and, instead, viewed Creeks as "unpredictable savages" who jeopardized Georgian expansion (141).

Crucially, Haynes asserts that Creek raids "reflected and amplified" the "paradox[ical]" tension in eighteenth-century Creek politics between town autonomy and a centralizing, "coalescing" nation (13, 86). Nationalist headmen and localized warriors agreed that sovereignty rested on land but diverged over how best to preserve land. From Escotchaby of Coweta to Alexander McGillivray of Little Tallassee, headmen spoke for the "nation" in negotiations with imperial, federal, and state authorities. By contrast, young men objected to nationalists' pretensions by frequently stealing property and infrequently killing white and black settlers. Still, Haynes bridges the archaeological and historical scholarship to prove that Creek patrollers clung to the "deep roots" of Mississippian traditions, such as gaining honors in war (139).

*Patrolling the Border* is a compact study of indigenous politics and cross-cultural relations that will spark debate in graduate courses on American Indian history, the American Revolution, and Southern history. The book's digital mapping tools, moreover, would work well in historical methods and historical geography courses. Although it is not always clear when border raids captured "popular sentiment" (158) in towns, provinces, or the nation, Haynes has advanced the scholarly discussion on violence and nation building in Southeastern Indian history.

Unsettling Mobility: Mediating Mi'kmaw Sovereignty in Post-contact Nova Scotia. By Michelle A. Lelièvre. (Tucson: University of Arizona Press, 2017. xix +257 pp., illustrations, acknowledgments, notes, references, index. $60.00 hardcover.)

Catherine M. Cameron, *University of Colorado, Boulder*

Michelle A. Lelièvre's aptly titled *Unsettling Mobility* characterizes human movement as far more than simply relocating from one place to another. Instead movement can *emplace* people on the lands across which they move and mediate social, political, and economic relations among diverse users of a landscape. This new take on mobility is developed here around a detailed study of the Mi'kmaw people, an indigenous group occupying the northeast shore of mainland Nova Scotia (Pictou Landing First Nation) and their peripatetic use of Maligomish, a small island just off the coast. Occupation of the island may extend back 1,500 years and today the Mi'kmaw consider it sacred. It contains ancient burial grounds, a cemetery with historic and recent burials, and the nineteenth-century Saint Anne's mission church where Mi'kmaw gather annually to celebrate Saint Anne's day.

Lelièvre uses ethnographic, archaeological, and historical data to explore the Mi'kmaw engagement with their ancestral lands and with the European institutions that eventually governed them. Lelièvre's close interactions with the contemporary Mi'kmaw people and her research into their recent and historic ancestors are central to the book. The book's introduction sets out the author's intention to offer an anthropological analysis of how movement has mediated sociopolitical relationships between Mi'kmaq people and the British Crown and Catholic Church. These institutions attempted to "civilize" the hunting and gathering Mi'kmaq by pinning them down in reserves. Lelièvre shows that by continuing to move across and use ancestral lands outside the reserves, the Mi'kmaq were engaging in acts of sovereignty and constituting themselves as political subjects. Furthermore, movement across Mi'kmaq traditional lands, as well as actions by the Church and Crown, served to emplace the Mi'kmaq on these lands. Not only did the Mi'kmaq continue to move, but representatives of the state and Church who attempted to manage them were also forced to be mobile.

Chapter 1 briefly reviews the appropriation of Mi'kmaq territory by European settlers and describes both the "sedentarist ideology" that pervaded in settlers' perceptions of their claims to the land and the history of

*Ethnohistory* 66:4 (October 2019)   DOI 10.1215/00141801-7683474
Copyright 2019 by American Society for Ethnohistory

this ideology in anthropological thought. The author's archaeological work on Maligomish consisted of excavations in a shell midden and a full-coverage survey of the island, work conducted in collaboration with Mi'kmaq people. Chapter 2 presents the result of the excavations by describing three points at which archaeological data and Mi'kmaw accounts of the midden intersect. Chapter 3 presents the results of the survey, enriched by a detailed description of Mi'kmaq dwellings derived from historic and contemporary sources. Using studies of individual family movement, as well as the survey data, Lelièvre shows the complexity of Mi'kmaq mobility, including their use of permanent and temporary structures.

The Mi'kmaq converted to Catholicism in the early seventeenth century and remained adherents even after the British takeover. Chapter 4 describes the annual Saint Anne's Day events on Maligomish that brings Mi'kmaq families on a pilgrimage to venerate this Catholic saint. Throughout their four-hundred-year involvement, the Church offered the Mi'kmaq only a "mission" here without a permanent priest; as a result, the Mi'kmaq modified Catholic practices, interpreting them in their own way. The Church eventually came to collude with the Crown in its administration of the Mi'kmaw.

The book's conclusion underscores the continued importance of mobility for First Nations people, describing long walks to political capitols by First Nation youth to force the state to redress its ongoing neglect of their people. In this last chapter Lelièvre's main point is underscored: mobility for First Nations people is a key aspect of their sociopolitical engagement. This is a book that will be enjoyed by anthropologists eager for new theories of mobility, as well as by historians and other scholars interested in the myriad aspects of postcolonial land use.

Illicit Love: Interracial Sex and Marriage in the United States and Australia.
By Ann McGrath. (Lincoln: University of Nebraska Press, 2015. xxxi+503
pp., illustrations, preface, acknowledgements, notes, bibliography, index.
$35.00 paper.)

Brandon Layton, *University of California, Davis*

In *Illicit Love: Interracial Sex and Marriage in the United States and Australia*, Ann McGrath offers a comparative study of intimate relations
between indigenous peoples and European colonizers in North America
and Australia. She focuses on two indigenous communities: the Cherokees
in the early nineteenth century and the aborigines of North Queensland
in the late nineteenth century. McGrath argues that although interracial
unions sometimes allowed indigenous communities greater influence in
white worlds, they were not solely pragmatic or strategic. Instead, intermarriage often derived from love, or "tender emotions." As love crossed socio-
cultural boundaries, it destabilized the social order imposed by colonizers.

McGrath articulates her argument most clearly in biographical chapters
on individual love stories. Chapter 1 examines the relationship between
Cherokee scholar Elias Boudinot and a nineteen-year-old white woman
from New England, Harriet Gold. Chapter 2 discusses an affair between
Methodist missionary Ernest Gribble and an aboriginal woman named
Jeannie. Chapter 4 focuses on fifty-year-old Cherokee chief John Ross
and his marriage to a sixteen-year-old white girl, Mary Bryan Stapler.
Given the age disparity, characterizing this latter relationship as "love," as
McGrath does, seems problematic. Yet overall, these personal accounts
reveal the emotions driving interracial relationships.

McGrath organizes her other chapters thematically, with particular
focus on attempts by indigenous communities and colonial authorities to
regulate intermarriage. For example, Cherokee leaders sought to limit the
ability of white men to marry into the nation and thus gain access to
valuable Cherokee lands. In Australia, aboriginal men sometimes resorted
to violence against whites who courted aboriginal women without following indigenous kinship practices. The American and British governments similarly passed laws forbidding intermarriage, viewing it as a threat
to the racial order they sought to establish.

Although McGrath's main arguments center around love and the
disruptive nature of intermarriage, she embraces the complex and even

*Ethnohistory* 66:4 (October 2019)   DOI 10.1215/00141801-7683492

contradictory aspects of cross-cultural romance. While such relationships could benefit indigenous communities, they could also further the goal of colonizers in assimilating and dispossessing Native peoples. Interracial sex was not always romantic either. It could derive from tender emotions, but as often, it manifested as sexual violence at the hands of the colonizer against indigenous women. Sexual relations between Euro-Americans and Natives always reflected a broader contest over power. Even consensual relationships opened debate on competing definitions of marriage, kinship, and sovereignty.

McGrath's juxtaposition of America and Australia allows her to tease out similarities and differences that a unifocal examination might overlook. McGrath contends that intermarriage functioned on what she terms the "marital middle ground," a space where Euro-American and indigenous partners created new, hybrid cultural forms (25). She borrows this concept from Richard White, but White regarded the middle ground as a temporary phenomenon during early colonialization, while McGrath views the marital middle ground as a more permanent institution.

At times McGrath unduly paints America and Australia as mirror settler-colonial images of one another. The case studies she chooses reveal significant differences: Cherokee men who married white women versus white men who married aborigines. Most intermarriage for the Cherokees occurred between white men and Indian women, but McGrath focuses on the few counter examples. These examples exist because the Cherokees of the early nineteenth century already had two centuries of interacting (and intermarrying) with Euro-Americans and had selectively embraced aspects of white culture. The Cherokees' earlier history receives limited treatment. Queensland aborigines were only just beginning to wrestle with colonialism, which led to a greater cultural gulf between them and their British colonizers.

Despite this shortcoming, McGrath unveils a complex history of intermarriage that is at once intimately personal and part of a much broader transnational, colonial story.

**Sea Otters: A History.** By Richard Ravalli. (Lincoln: University of Nebraska Press, 2018. xxiv + 189 pp., illustrations, acknowledgements, appendices, notes, bibliography, index. $45.00 cloth.)

John Ryan Fischer, *University of Wisconsin–River Falls*

Adele Ogden's 1941 *The California Sea Otter Trade, 1784–1848* has provided the first and last word on its subject for generations. Ogden's research was extensive, but Richard Ravalli's *Sea Otters* is a welcome addition that integrates new historiography and methods from environmental history, while casting the otter fur trade as a trans-Pacific event. Ravalli notes that the animals, of the species *Enhydra lustis*, have recently become media darlings for their adorable looks and behavior, but the earlier exploitation of their furs by Russian, Japanese, Spanish, English, and US hunters played an important role in the development of trans-Pacific economic links.

Ravalli organizes the book chronologically and places much of its focus throughout on the imperial rivalries that the desirability of otter furs encouraged. The first chapter shows how Russia's eastern expansion and increased trade with China in the 1700s led to exploitation of the animals in that period and contestation of the Kuril Islands with Japan. Ainu people in the region often found themselves in the middle of this dispute, and both sides exploited their labor in the fur trade. In the second chapter, Ravalli traces Russian fur hunters, or *promyshlenniki*, to the west coast of North America where they prompted rivalry with the Spanish and their colonization of Upper California. The third chapter covers the heavy involvement of traders from New England along the California coast in the nineteenth century. The peak of the trade in the mid-nineteenth century, covered in chapter 4, led to widespread otter population declines, though Ravalli does note that other ecological factors could have played a role. This led to the first international conservation measures for the species, culminating in an international treaty in 1911. Finally, chapter 5 explores post–World War II conservation efforts, including anti–nuclear testing arguments and species rediscovery/recolonization on some Pacific coasts.

Ravalli's book is brief, and it often feels that we are only getting a tantalizing glimpse of rich topics for research. For instance, early conservation efforts on the Pribolof Islands led to concerns about indigenous Aleuts' economic welfare, which was firmly tied to the hunt. While Ravalli is always cognizant of the central place that indigenous peoples, including

*Ethnohistory* 66:4 (October 2019)   DOI 10.1215/00141801-7683510
Copyright 2019 by American Society for Ethnohistory

Ainu, Aleuts, and California Indians, had in the fur trade, his coverage of the social and cultural impacts of the trade on them is also brief and glancing. The book's greatest strength is its geographic comprehensiveness, and Ravalli frames it as a synthesis of studies from different Pacific regions. The focus on sources available in English and the study's brevity mean that there is probably further exploration to do on the fur trade in Japanese and Russian waters, as well as in North American waters plied by non-English speakers.

Ravalli skillfully integrates ecological and biological research on the animals. He also touches on the strong tendency humans have to anthropomorphize otters and focus on their cuteness, and he discusses biologists' critiques of this tendency. Again, it feels like there are rich opportunities to explore this further and elaborate on the significant change in perceptions of the animals as they moved from an exploited resource to social media stars.

Overall, this book is a rich starting point, and scholars exploring the sea otter trade or the eighteenth- and nineteenth-century trans-Pacific economy will find plenty of useful information. *Ethnohistory* readers may be disappointed by the shallow treatment that indigenous workers receive, but this book does provide useful background that could help to underwrite deeper explorations. Reprints of Adele Ogden's helpful catalogs of otter trade ships in California in the appendices also add to the book's utility.

Converting the Rosebud: Catholic Mission and the Lakotas, 1886–1916.
By Harvey Markowitz. (Norman: University of Oklahoma Press, 2018.
320 pp., preface, acknowledgments, illustrations, notes, bibliography, and
index. $34.95 hardcover.)

David C. Posthumus, *University of South Dakota*

Harvey Markowitz's *Converting the Rosebud: Catholic Mission and the
Lakotas, 1886–1916* provides a refreshing and enjoyable read and a much-
needed addition and update to the Christian-mission literature in Native
North America. For me, this is the most usable and accessible work of its
kind since Sister Mary Claudia Duratschek's important work *Crusading
along Sioux Trails: A History of the Catholic Indian Missions of South
Dakota* (1947). Markowitz's project is more ambitious and comprehensive,
and it is definitely a valuable contribution, suited to scholars, students, and
a wider general audience alike.

   More than just a strict history of the Catholic mission among the
Lakotas, *Converting the Rosebud* is a sweeping and enthralling epic exploring Lakota relations with the US federal government and its missioniz-
ing, "civilizing," and educating branches. It is a marvelously researched and
nuanced history of Lakota-white relations through the lens of the Catholic
mission and the personalities comprising it. Weaving together insights on
treaties, federal Indian policy, and Indian education, Markowitz provides
plenty of background for students, scholars, and general readers to understand the complex and evolving social and political dynamics of missionization in Sioux Country. This book also provides a fascinating and highly
accessible window into political tensions between Catholics and the federal
government, Catholics and the Bureau of Indian Affairs, and Catholics and
Protestant sects, who competed for Native souls and the (federal) monies
needed to keep their operations afloat.

   Markowitz also explores more generally the Lakota encounter with
Western religious traditions and philosophy and how the Lakotas were active
agents in this history, adopting and indigenizing ideas from Catholicism
as they suited their material needs and spiritual beliefs, while preserving
their traditional beliefs, values, and ritual practice. This ancient indigenous religious foundation was vastly different from Western Judeo-Christian
traditions, but there were key ideas, such as *wakȟáŋ* (mystery, spiritual power), that Lakotas actively drew on to build a theosophical bridge

*Ethnohistory* 66:4 (October 2019)   DOI 10.1215/00141801-7683528
Copyright 2019 by American Society for Ethnohistory

between the two traditions or roads. The unevenness of missionization among the Lakotas is another key point explored here, demonstrating the varied responses, reactions, and adaptations to Catholicism in a complex society and historical epoch.

As a scholar of Lakota culture and ceremonial life, I felt that Markowitz articulated and fleshed out some important themes that no one had fully explored until this work. Specifically, Markowitz highlights the importance of understanding the Saint Joseph and Saint Mary Societies and native catechists in the broader unfolding of the Catholic mission at Rosebud. He also highlights the (subversive) role of Fourth of July celebrations as a more-or-less covert means to gather socially and perpetuate Lakota cultural traditions, in spite of a government ban on practicing Lakota spirituality, giveaways, mourning practices, or any other expressions of "being Indian." Grappling with these underappreciated aspects of the history of missionization makes this book stand out as a distinctive contribution.

*Converting the Rosebud* is now the go-to source on the history of (Catholic) missionization among the Lakotas. This is a dark history in many ways, but one that must be explored and understood. It contributes to many disciplines, including anthropology, history, Native American studies, Lakota studies, and religious studies. This book would be great for the classroom as well as the scholar's bookshelf, and it is a real page-turner, which isn't always the case with scholarly works. Markowitz succeeds brilliantly here in bringing this complex and important story to a wider audience and doing so in an exemplary and compelling way.

EXTENT AND NATURE OF CIRCULATION: Average number of copies of each issue published during the preceding twelve months; (A) total number of copies printed, 735; (B.1) paid/requested mail subscriptions, 385; (B.4) Paid distribution by other classes, 0; (C) total paid/requested circulation, 385; (D.1) samples, complimentary, and other nonrequested copies, 24.5; (D.4) nonrequested copies distributed through outside the mail, 63; (E) total nonrequested distribution (sum of D.1 & D.4), 87.5; (F) total distribution (sum of C & E), 472.5; (G) copies not distributed (office use, leftover, unaccounted, spoiled after printing, returns from news agents), 262.5; (H) total (sum of F & G), 735.

Actual number of copies of a single issue published nearest to filing date: (A) total number of copies printed, 555; (B.1) paid/requested mail subscriptions, 430; (B.4) Paid distribution by other classes, 0; (C) total paid/requested circulation, 430; (D.1) samples, complimentary, and other nonrequested copies, 4; (D.4) nonrequested copies distributed through outside the mail, 45; (E) total nonrequested distribution (sum of D.1 & D.4), 49; (F) total distribution (sum of C & E), 479; (G) copies not distributed (office use, leftover, unaccounted, spoiled after printing, returns from news agents), 76; (H) total (sum of F & G), 555.

## History of the Chichimeca Nation
*Don Fernando de Alva Ixtlilxochitl's*
*SeventeethCentury Chronicle of Ancient Mexico*
Translated and edited by Amber Brian, Bradley Benton, Peter B. Villella, and Pablo García Loaeza

Here for the first time in English translation, is one of the liveliest, most accessible, and most influential accounts of the rise and fall of Aztec Mexico derived from indigenous sources and memories and written from a native perspective.

................................................................................

$60.00 HARDCOVER · $29.95 PAPERBACK · 352 PAGES · 24 B&W ILLUS.

## Making a Difference
*My Fight for Native Rights and Social Justice*
By Ada Deer with Theda Perdue

This stirring memoir is the story of Ada Deer, the first woman to serve as head of the Bureau of Indian Affairs. She narrates the first eighty three years of her life, which are characterized by her tireless campaigns to reverse the forced termination of the Menominee tribe and to ensure sovereignty and self-determination for all tribes.

................................................................................

$26.95 HARDCOVER · 232 PAGES · 13 B&W ILLUS.

## Records of the Moravians among the Cherokees
*Volume Eight: In Their Own Voice—"Power to Remove"*
Edited by Richard W. Starbuck

The subtitle In Their Own Voice—"Power to Remove" sets the tension-filled tone of Volume 8 of Records of the Moravians among the Cherokees. In the brief span of just two and a half years, 1828 to July 1830, events take place that seal the fate of the Cherokees east of the Mississippi.

................................................................................

$40.00 HARDCOVER · 544 PAGES · 112 B&W ILLUS.

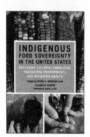

## Indigenous Food Sovereignty in the United States
*Restoring Cultural Knowledge, Protecting*
*Environments, and Regaining Health*
Edited by Devon A. Mihesuah and Elizabeth Hoover

Centuries of colonization and other factors have disrupted indigenous communities' ability to control their own food systems. This volume explores the meaning and importance of food sovereignty for Native peoples in the United States.

................................................................................

$29.95 PAPERBACK · 390 PAGES · 17 B&W ILLUS.

**UNIVERSITY OF OKLAHOMA PRESS**

1 800 848 6224 EXT.1 · OUPRESS.COM
CONNECT WITH US

THE UNIVERSITY OF OKLAHOMA IS AN EQUAL OPPORTUNITY INSTITUTION. WWW.OU.EDU/EOO